The
Reading/Writing
Teacher's
Companion

DISCOVER
YOUR OWN
LITERACY

The
Reading/Writing
Teacher's
Companion

Investigate Nonfiction
Experiment with Fiction
Discover Your Own Literacy
Build a Literate Classroom
Explore Poetry (forthcoming)

The
Reading/Writing
Teacher's
Companion

DISCOVER
YOUR OWN
LITERACY

Donald H. Graves

HEINEMANN
Portsmouth, NH

IRWIN PUBLISHING
Toronto, Canada

Heinemann

A division of Reed Publishing (USA), Inc.

361 Hanover Street, Portsmouth, NH 03801-3912

Offices and agents throughout the world

Published simultaneously in Canada by

Irwin Publishing

1800 Steeles Avenue West   Concord, Ontario, Canada L4K 2P3

The author and publisher wish to thank the following for permission to reprint previously published material:

Pages 90–91: Excerpt from *The Power of Myth* by Joseph Campbell and Bill Moyers. Copyright © 1988 by Apostrophe S Productions, Inc. and Bill Moyers and Alfred van der Mack Editions, Inc. for itself and the estate of Joseph Campbell. Reprinted by permission of Doubleday, a division of Bantam, Doubleday, Dell Publishing Group, Inc.

Every effort has been made to contact the copyright holders for permission to reprint borrowed material. We regret any oversights that may have occurred and would be happy to rectify them in future printings of this work.

Library of Congress Cataloging-in-Publication Data

Graves, Donald H.
Discover your own literacy / Donald H. Graves.
  p. cm.—(Reading/writing teacher's companion)
Includes bibliographical references and index.
ISBN 0-435-08487-9
1. Language arts (Elementary) 2. Language arts teachers—In-service training. I. Title. II. Series.
LB1576.G7273 1990
372.6—dc20   89-36848
                                                    CIP

Canadian Cataloguing in Publication Data

Graves, Donald H.
  Discover your own literacy

(The Reading/writing teacher's companion)
Includes bibliographical references.
ISBN 0-7725-1723-1

1. Creative writing (Elementary education)—Study and teaching. 2. Reading (Elementary). 3. Language arts (Elementary). I. Title. II. Series: Graves, Donald H. The reading/writing teacher's companion.

LB1576.G72 1990   372.6′23   C89-094871-2

Designed by Wladislaw Finne.
Back-cover photo by Mekeel McBride.
Printed in the United States of America.
10 9 8 7 6 5 4 3

To
Classroom Teachers

---

*Who continue to be
my first teachers*

contents

Action: Form a Group to Share Books.
Final Reflection

about this series

Reading and writing are both composing processes. History shows they have been kept apart. This series, The Reading/Writing Teacher's Companion, brings them together. With these books as a guide, you can explore the richness of reading and writing for yourself and for children. You can improve your own listening, experiment with learning, and recognize children's potential in reading and writing. Five books will make up the series:

- *Investigate Nonfiction.*
- *Experiment with Fiction.*
- *Discover Your Own Literacy.*
- *Build a Literate Classroom.*
- *Explore Poetry.*

The approach to teaching and learning is basically the same in all five books, although each stands alone in its focus. All five emphasize a learning style that immediately engages you in trying literacy for yourself, then the children. So much of learning is, and ought to be, experimental. A series of "Actions," experiments for personal growth and discovery in the classroom, are highlighted in the text to help you develop the kind of literate classroom you want. The Actions are ordered in such a way that you will gradually become aware of children's growing independence in some aspect of literacy. In all five books I'll be trying the experiments right along with you.

The five books stress learning within a literate community. Reading and writing are social acts in which children and teachers together share the books and authors they enjoy and their own composing in the various genres. Make no mistake, individuals are important, but good classrooms have always stressed group as well as individual responsibility.

The books also stress the importance of your own learning within a community. When you try the Actions and enter into new experiments with your teaching, you ought to consider reading and learning with colleagues in order to maximize your own efforts to grow as a professional.

acknowl-edgments

This book represents more than a decade of observing, learning, and working with classroom teachers. It is classroom teachers who have taught me the importance of reading and writing in their own lives as the base from which good teaching comes. It is their literacy and commitment to the profession that makes the difference in the classroom. This book is dedicated to classroom teachers everywhere who work day by day, year after year, with a vision for their children that nearly always exceeds that of persons outside their classrooms.

The list of teachers who have helped me is almost too long to mention, but some stand out immediately: Mary Ellen Giacobbe, Judy Egan, Ellen Blackburn Karelitz, Pat McLure, Leslie Funkhouser, Janice Roberts, Phyllis Kinzie, Nancie Atwell, Susan Stires, Jack Wilde, Carol Avery, Paula Flemming, Terri Moher, Tom Romano, Peter Schiot, and Linda Rief.

For three years (1986–89) our research team, led by Jane Hansen, has worked at Stratham Memorial School. Bill Wansart, Professor of Learning Disabilities, joined the team in the second year and helped us to see the potential of children with special needs. The Stratham teachers taught me the power of the literate community. That is, they have shown me how teachers pull together to help each other in literate endeavors. Their view of the literate life is rich enough to support diverse approaches to working with children. They taught me that it is their own engagement with books and writing that has opened the door to new standards of excellence in the children. All of the Stratham teachers helped. Many of them are quoted in this book, especially in Chapter 4. I am indebted to David Michaud and Katie Kramer, who were principals during the study.

I am grateful for the support of Jane Hansen, my colleague in research for the past eight years. She has responded to each chapter with helpful suggestions and encouragement. But it is her own reading and writing, the articles and books she pushes my way as well as the drafts of her own writing, that enrich my own climate and spur me on to continued work. Jane has that knack of establishing literate communities wherever she works. I am fortunate to be part of that community.

I am also fortunate to be part of a community of doctoral students who provide still another edge to literate challenge. For the last five years they have extended my own reading, writing, and thinking. Their reading is varied and voracious. "Have you read this?" is a familiar question. The following doctoral students, present and former, have been especially helpful in providing that literate community: Lorri Neilsen, Mary Ellen Macmillan, Ruth Hubbard, Brenda Miller Power, Tom Romano, Dan Ling Fu, Bonnie Sunstein, Tim Rynkofs, Elizabeth Chiseri Strater, Judy Fueyo, Mary Comstock, Ann Vibert, Jay Simmons, Dan Seger, Meg Peterson, and Peggy Murray.

Don Murray has helped. Our daily discussions about writing and reading, whether it is fiction, poetry, or nonfiction, provide the necessary backdrop for my own thinking and writing. Murray's daily practice of his craft naturally follows the questions he asks of others. His "What's new?" continues to open a world of detail that might otherwise go unnoticed.

I am indebted to Nancie Atwell, the quintessential literate teacher. She, more than any other teacher, has demonstrated the powerful influence a teacher who reads, writes, and cares can have on her students. She has showed so many teachers and professors like myself just what is possible for students. I also thank her for her many responses to the chapters in this book and the entire Reading/Writing Teacher's Companion series.

Philippa Stratton, Editor-in-Chief at Heinemann Educational Books, has provided guidance for this five-book series. The series began as only one book four years ago, *The Writing Teacher's Companion*. Through Philippa's persistent logic and perception of the field of literacy, the project slowly grew from one book, to two, then to five. I am grateful for her support and patience, and for my education as a writer.

Donna Bouvier, Manager of Editing and Production at Heinemann, saw the manuscript through to polished form. There are literally hundreds of niggling details that demand attention in the final phases of carrying a book through to finished product. The difference between a polished, pleasing book and a publication marred by a few blatant errors is as close as a few seconds of oversight. Her calm, agreeable manner in seeing through the entire series has made it so easy for me to concentrate on the text at hand.

My wife, Betty, has participated in this book more than usual. She read and she taught. Betty demonstrated her perceptive reading of a section of Joseph Campbell's *The Power of Myth*, and she taught me how to use the sewing machine, as I note in Chapter 6. She has also read each of the chapters as I completed them, made suggestions, and gave me encouragement to carry on through the writing of this long series. I simply could not have finished the work without her.

1

discover your own literacy

"All right," Mary Ann Wessells challenges her fifth-grade class, "tell me why there is so much violence in your fiction." The class is gathered on the floor in a corner of the room. The children are used to such meetings and reply in a rapid-fire, direct manner. They know from their teacher's question that she doesn't know the answer.

"We aren't really violent, Ms. Wessells."

"We're just playing; we aren't serious about it."

"Well, it still bothers me. We need to talk about it some more," Mary Ann replies. Big questions, frank questions, are the modus operandi in this classroom. Since Mary Ann Wessells discovered her own literacy, like many teachers across the United States and abroad, the quality of learning, literacy, and exchange in her classroom has changed, as it has in thousands of other classrooms as well. The teachers' discovery of literacy has paralleled that of their students. But the turnaround was possible only when teachers decided to do something about their own literate engagement.

For many, the decision to take charge of their own literacy resulted from a dissatisfaction that had been building for years. Tired of impersonal curriculum guides that spelled out detailed skills for appropriate months at specific grade levels, of end-of-book tests, dull and lifeless textbook language, and uninformed classroom observations and evaluations, these teachers said, "Enough. We're going to do something about it . . . and we're the only ones who can." Most of them can almost remember the moment when they started on a new road to literacy, leaving behind a rather boring professional life devoid of enthusiasm.

Taking charge meant a new kind of engagement with the world, not just a turnaround in the classroom. The urge to learn from trade books, newspapers, friends, shopkeepers, their own children at home, and their students in school became paramount. These teachers listen and question. They recognize their own authority to learn and then to act. Mary Ann Wessells

1

asked her students about the violence in their fiction because she wanted to know exactly what they thought. The violence bothered her, but she was also genuinely curious about their reasons. But her questions are not just for the classroom; she also asks questions at faculty and curriculum meetings.

For Mary Ann, the change began in a writing course six years ago. "I took the plunge. It was terrifying. I literally shook during my first assignment. My history as a writer gave me no encouragement." The remarkable part of the writing course was not the writing as much as it was the listening required in writing conferences.

MARY ANN: I began with the writing process and the conferences that went with it. I started listening in the beginning because it was a necessary part of the teaching. I became very aware that they [the children] had fascinating things to say and also unique ways of doing or saying things. And I became aware of the fact that teachers have to be good listeners. I wanted my students to be good listeners, so I figured I had to also. The more I listen, the more I learn, and then it becomes more interesting. Every group is a new group. Every year is new. You'll never get bored. You'll never find them the same.

Learning to listen meant that Mary Ann asked bigger questions in order to learn still more about what the children meant when they wrote and spoke. Gradually, as Mary Ann improved her listening literacy, she became more knowledgeable about what her children knew and how they knew it. Not only was she gathering firsthand information, she also wrote about what she was learning and shared her data at faculty meetings. Eventually she made presentations at national conventions. Her questions and the authority of her own information expanded her professional world.

Although Mary Ann made an individual decision to change

her approach to teaching, she also found other teachers who were similarly concerned about literacy for children. As a teacher at Stratham Memorial School in Stratham, New Hampshire, she now shares stories, books, writing, and teaching strategies with a host of other professionals. She has made it a point to find teachers with whom she can share.

MARY ANN: And by listening I've been able to change the way the children use their time. The children are able to take responsibility in a different way. First, they use time and content more responsibly. I used to be a kind of mechanical teacher: put the vocabulary words on the board, pass out ditto sheets, read the story of the day, meet with small groups in rotation, and introduce a new skill. Now they use a straight block of time on their own, with thirty minutes for their reading, thirty minutes for their writing, and other time for sharing, helping each other, and having conferences in small groups and with me individually.

"I have to tell you I was ready to quit teaching before I got into this," Mary Ann went on. "The other day some of the children were joking and saying, 'If you had a million dollars you wouldn't have to teach any more,' and I said, 'Oh, I'd have to teach; I'll never stop.' A few years back I would have left."

When Mary Ann speaks of the "fun of teaching," she speaks of it in terms of what she does both in and out of school. As I listen to her explanation I begin to realize that one cannot be separated from the other:

MARY ANN: Outside of school I used to spend a lot of time correcting. In personal terms, I didn't have time for myself. What's happened, what's changed is that I spend less time on that kind of schoolwork. I'm trying to carry a process approach into science and social studies. As I'm doing that I'm eliminating a lot of paperwork. What I'm doing now is spending time with reading journals, usually five a day. I look over writing folders. I see a lot [of folders and journals] in the day, but I do more after school.

And I spend more time writing myself. I didn't do that before at all. Also, interestingly enough, I'm doing more professional reading. I'm trying to find out how other people are doing it. Then there's my own personal, fun reading. And part of my planning time is spent trying to find different ways to learn and evaluate more. What I was doing before was mechanical, rote, scut work that didn't tell anything about the children.

Outside of school there has been more time to study at the university, and I find it easier now to fit in my aerobics, weights, and running. There's more of a place for *me* now. And I'm moving out there by doing workshops and presentations. It's all learning. There's more time for learning, both in class with the children and outside.

Mary Ann has found that the more responsibility she gives to the children in terms of both time and choice, the more effective she can be in evaluating what they are doing. She can stand back and see how to teach instead of spending endless hours correcting. She has had more time to diversify her interests outside of school, and this, in turn, has given her a different kind of energy in the classroom. She comes to school feeling energetic and leaves feeling energetic because she and the children have forged a partnership in their enjoyment of learning.

Mary Ann reads and writes with the children. She reads aloud books that she likes. This year she read *A Wrinkle in Time, A Wind in the Door, Bridge to Terabithia, The B.F.G., The Computer Nut,* and *The Legend of Sleepy Hollow.* Now she is reading scary short stories. The children see her learn as they respond to her writing, which she shares with them in class.

WRITE WITH YOUR
STUDENTS

Linda Rief, a middle school teacher in Durham, New Hampshire, asks her students big questions in the context of real situations. Linda reads and writes with her students about the elderly. They visit elderly people in nursing homes, correspond with them, and write about their experiences. The students read essays, poetry, and fiction as background for their work with the elderly and their own attempts to understand another generation. And Linda does the work right along with them. They encounter big questions together in the course of their work: What about death? Are we fair to the elderly? What should we be doing? Does the government care? What can we learn from them? It is these kinds of questions, the honest questions that follow encounters with real people, that inspire writing and reading.

Janet Moore, one of Linda's students, wrote a poem from the viewpoint of a woman she visited in a nursing home, because she thought it would help her to understand the woman's world.

A quiet, sunny day
walking through the breezeway, the canaries
caught my eye like earrings on a child
My books in hand
my cat Shar followed me
his tail straight up and blue eyes intense
Walking through the garden, the lush green
wet my hands and the scent of the lilies
of the valley was thick in my head
The stately blue spruce stood in the
middle of the rock garden like a soldier
in the midst of family
I stopped to look
then continued on my way to sit
under the tree
Shar came right up next to me

His bright cat eyes closed against the sun
and he rubbed his silky cheek against my knee
His long sea-black fur brushed softly
against my fingers
His paws reached to my chest and felt
like stamps on a soft envelope
His twenty pounds curled itself upon my chest
I breathed in and began to read

And now, under that stately tree,
there is a box
entwined in the arms of the roots
secured by the earth
In it is my sunny day
only it's black as night
I am three thousand miles away
but Shar's blue eyes still look at me
on a sunny day.

Janet Moore

Linda wrote a poem along with the class, struggling with her own perceptions and feelings about the woman she visits at the nursing home:

TRYING TO REMEMBER

"My memory is one . . . loud . . . void . . ."
Margaret chuckles softly.

Nothing moves but her arm, mechanically,
like a water-wheel turning from her lap.

She clutches the edge
of a blue, terrycloth bib,
smoothing the corners
until they all touch
like rabbit's noses.

Two silver wedding bands drift
on parchment sticks,
　　as Margaret's arm moves up, and down, back,
　　　　and forth,
　　　　　　in the sign of a cross.
"Where are you from?" I ask.
Faded blue eyes dart to my words.
Her hand cups her chin.
One finger slowly caresses
the side of her nose,
and her vacant stare
returns my question.
She folds her bib again, all corners matching,
then spreads the towel across her mouth
and nose like an oxygen mask.
"Margaret?" I whisper. "Are you sleeping?"
"I'm trying to remember . . ." she exhales,
　　and slowly turns out another cross.
　　　　　　　　　　　　　　　　　Linda Rief

Linda Rief has written and read her way into an unusual professional career. She explains how it began:

LINDA: I started eight years ago by working as an aide with classroom teachers. I remember I always wanted to know what the kids knew. I talked with them a lot and found out what they could do. I wanted them to get involved with real reading and writing, doing it for themselves.

Well before taking any courses Linda focused on children and finding out what they knew. She had a strong desire for them to become independent (independent people like Linda tend to want to help others know the same independence). Such words and phrases as "connect with life," "trust," "expect," "initiative," and "kids know something" dot her explanations of what she wants for herself and for children.

After two years of working as an aide, Linda took a writing course that meshed with these hopes.

LINDA: I was scared to death. I never expected to write in a writing course. The class laughed when I wrote a piece about my car at a dump. It didn't just convey a message but an emotion. You can cause someone to react and that's when I wanted it for kids. That dump piece was the beginning of myself as a writer.

Within a few years Linda was far enough along in working toward a master's degree to receive a position as an English teacher.

LINDA: I started out doing what other teachers said I should be doing. I started out with units. Over time I've just weeded out units [and now I give kids] real choice [in their] writing. I couldn't let go of things all at once. I offered them topics. I wasn't comfortable that they really knew what to write about. I needed more time to let them come up with their own topics. I was trusting them, but not nearly enough. I wasn't trusting myself in the sense that I had to be accountable to someone for what I was doing. I had to have some test and skill results of what the kids were doing. I hadn't been doing enough writing myself to know what a real writer does. I think I was relying on my past history with teachers myself. I waited for their topics, waited for the teacher to fix it, recopied their corrections, then handed it in for a grade. I knew that wasn't right, because I never felt like a writer when I wrote under those conditions. I kept taking courses to find out what worked for me as a writer. Writing is both fun and very important for me now, and that's what I want for my students.

Each year Linda continued to take courses in poetry, research in the teaching of writing, and still more courses in writing. Although these courses put some emphasis on the teaching of writing, in actuality she studied in order to learn more about writing from the inside. She worked with writers herself and later shared with her students what worked for her in her own writing.

Linda wrote in class along with her students throughout the school year. At the end of the year when she asked her students what helped them most with their writing, they responded: "You wrote with us."

LINDA: They would talk about the types of writing I'd share with them. I'd share anything—things emotional for me, sad things that I would've had a hard time dealing with. I wanted them to know I trusted them to respond in the right way. The more serious I got, the more serious they got, whether it was a poem about my mother's death or an educational article. They were so serious, so sophisticated. I kept on doing that with them. I trusted them completely to help me as a writer. I used their suggestions. They'd say, "I don't want to hurt your feelings, but didn't you use those words a little too often?" They could focus and cut through the emotion of a piece.

When teachers like Linda ask big questions and deal with them honestly, students do too. And Linda asks questions that relate to her students' experience, not relying on textbooks to anticipate the issues that concern young adolescents.

LINDA: So teaching is making connections. That's what I think it is. It is making connections with their lives, things that are real. When you read someone else's contrived questions, they just don't make sense. There's no thinking. You try to think of what the textbook writer wanted; there's no connection with your own life. There are questions there, but they can't connect with the lives of my students.

Linda published her first article in *Learning* in 1984. She has since published articles in *Language Arts, English Journal,* and *Business Digest* and chapters in several books. Initially Linda held back on writing for publication, reasoning as many teachers do, "I had the feeling it had all been said before." But publication affirmed the importance of her own thinking and changed her views about student publication: "I realized that if I could publish, the kids could publish what they were saying. They could share beyond their own classroom." Now they have published articles in such journals as *Merlin's Pen, Aegis,* and *Current Events* and received awards from *Scholastic Magazine.* The editor of *Merlin's Pen* wrote to Linda last year.

From the most recent Oyster River manuscripts (nine or ten pieces), I accepted one for publication, requested that three or four be revised again, and rejected the rest. Remarkable! Five pieces selected for revision or acceptance—from a total of ten contributions— represents a singular achievement. Five pieces of this caliber in 100 is the norm! Your instructional methods are working. All ten of the pieces stood out for their specificity, their control, and their freshness.

Freshness, specificity, and control are a result of the work in her classroom, where students refine their language in answer to their own big questions. Not all students publish, nor are all students accomplished writers, but they do face real issues. Here is Sean's piece about his father and the Vietnam War.

MY DAD IN THE VIETNAM WAR

This story is really hard for me to write. Its about my Dad who was in the Vietnam War. All the terrible things that happened. How he lost really good friends. Or about one day when my Dad was in a

Bar. And some kid rolled a live grenade in. It lucky did not exsplode. Or how he would be walking down the street and a Religous monk who had drenched himself with gasoline would light a match and burn himself to death just because he was protesting. This year at my Dads birthday, my sister andher friends bought my Dad a book on the Vietnam war. My Dad was happy and sad at the sametime. My Dad didn't want to talk about it because he had too maney bad feelings, Someday when my Dad can talk about it I hope he talks to me.

While Linda was focusing on her children's writing, she now realizes that she was neglecting their reading. In fact, she hardly read at all herself. But her personal reading and her teaching of reading turned around during a summer course with Mary Ellen Giacobbe three years ago:

LINDA: It started when Mary Ellen Giacobbe asked us to bring five books to her course. I couldn't find five books I had read because I'd focused so much on writing. What had we been reading in class? They were pieces out of anthologies. I wanted [the children] to read their own books, but I had none to offer them. I had no paperbacks in the classroom. I expected them to find books without any help. I didn't give them time to talk about books or about how you even find a book to read. All Mary Ellen asked was to bring our five favorite books. It really scared me. I was the reading teacher, but I wasn't reading because I didn't have time.

Now she makes time for reading. This year she spent her entire budget to put an additional two hundred books in her class-room. She selected titles after careful consultation with her students, who now read as eagerly as they write. The children requested a wide range of books, from *The Velveteen Rabbit* by Margery Williams to *Man's Search for Meaning* by Viktor Frankl.

Other books they wished to have in their classroom were by Judy Blume, S. E. Hinton, J. R. R. Tolkien, Jack London, and Farley Mowat.

Linda Rief, like Mary Ann Wessells, experienced an explosion of reading in her own life. Now she reads to keep up with the authors the children read, and for her own pleasure she is currently reading "everything Ann Tyler has written, poetry by Sharon Olds, William Stafford, Linda Pastan, Maxine Kumin, and Annie Dillard, and *Fallen Angels* by Walter D. Myers."

FINAL REFLECTION   Both Mary Ann Wessells and Linda Rief are engaged in a personal and professional journey: the two aspects cannot be separated. Although each believed her students knew things that would help her in her teaching, their histories as teachers and the way they taught made it difficult for them to get started. But when listening and literacy became inextricably intertwined, the process of discovering their own literacy began. Mary Ann began by listening to her students in writing conferences, mostly because it was "what I was supposed to do," Linda by becoming aware of the power of her own writing.

As they listened to their students, questions arose that became a natural part of their teaching and learning. "Why do you use so much violence in your writing?" "What about war?" "What can we do to understand the elderly?" "I'm not sure whether this lead works; what do you think?" Such questions don't have prepackaged answers. Mary Ann and Linda ask them because they don't know the answers, because they want to know—for themselves as much as for the children.

When Mary Ann and Linda speak about discovering their own literacy through writing, they both mention their fear. Neither of them began the journey on secure ground. It wasn't long, however, before they found out that their words affected other people, and as they saw the worth of writing for themselves and understood the process from the inside, they were able to challenge their students more effectively. Although each took writing courses, the experience of writing extended beyond the end of the course to become an essential part of how they learned with their students.

Neither Mary Ann nor Linda discovered reading for herself until she had explored writing. Often, school traditions and curriculum barriers make it difficult for teachers to change their reading programs. Previously, Mary Ann had used basals in her classroom and Linda, anthologies; neither of them made books the focus of her own reading. We underestimate the power that school curricula have on our own literacy. When Mary Ann and Linda allowed their students to move on to trade books, they discovered reading for themselves, right along with their students.

The initiative of these two teachers is striking. They didn't wait for an administrative directive or rely on a curriculum manual or search for the right textbook and teacher's guide. They knew they wanted to learn from their students, and they began by simultaneously listening to their students and learning to recognize their own voices in writing and reading. The source of their energy and the inspiration for their decisions were the students themselves. And just as the quality of their students' literacy has risen to an exceptional degree as a result, their own literacy has been encouraged in equally remarkable ways.

take the initiative

Professionals are people who make decisions. Literate professionals make decisions about their own literacy and the literacy of the children they teach. This book is about making the kinds of decisions that produce changes in your own personal literacy. In the classrooms of both Linda Rief and Mary Ann Wessells, and in the countless classrooms where I have seen students advance beyond the usual reading and writing program, significant change began when teachers rediscovered their own literacy.

Because it is difficult for me to anticipate the best starting point for each reader, I will provide a series of Actions through which you can experiment with new approaches to enjoying your own literacy. You will experiment so that each of the Actions ultimately becomes your own and works well with the other successful procedures you have brought into your teaching repertoire. Just where you start is up to you—as it should be. That will be your first decision. I suggest that you look over the chapter summaries that follow, keeping in mind your interests and what you consider your strongest suits in teaching. Your main focus will be on the experiment at hand.

The decision to try something new actually involves two dimensions—saying "yes" and saying "no." Sometimes decisions like this don't work because we fail to realize how much they affect the other areas of our lives. We all have established routines and rhythms, and the decision to experiment with writing or reading affects the other things we do. Most of the time we are unaware of what we say "no" to, believing that we have an infinite amount of time, and that something new can always be added. But disciplined, hardworking people, with well-tested routines, know that this is not so. At the same time, we *can* improve on the way we use our time.

THE EXPERIMENTS   Each of the following chapter summaries describes a particular kind of involvement as well as the rationale for including this approach in your teaching repertoire. If you wish, read through

15

all four before you start and then decide which one fits you best. The Actions in these chapters do not imply a progression. You can proceed in any order you choose, and all overlap with other Actions.

Chapter three:
Write with children

Your own demonstration of literacy through writing and reading sets the tone for your students' inquiry and reflection. You may wonder how you can find the class time to write with the children or even to make writing part of your own life. In approaching this problem, I have experimented with something I call a "literate occasion," in which I write for five to ten minutes about something in the classroom or in my own life that lends itself to writing. The key is to sketch in as many details as possible. Sometimes you will be able to do this during the school day with the children, but most of the time you will write outside of school. Writing in detail not only enhances your own life as you find out what writing can do, but it also helps you to understand what the children in your classroom are doing when they write. In Chapter 3 you will discover how "literate occasions" can become a way of living and learning. If you have already done some writing, this is an easy way to practice the discipline. If you have wanted to open the door to writing in your own life, literate occasions provide a way to get started.

Chapter four:
Read with children

As you pursue a reading life of your own and share your reading with others, you will want to make changes in your classroom. Chapter 4 lists Actions that provide many entry points to help you get back into doing more reading for yourself. Although learning how to read and discuss the thoughts and ideas contained in books is a very natural activity, we have made it far more complicated than it needs to be. This chapter describes ways for you to share books, read aloud, and connect reading with writing using children's literature as the basis of the reading program. You will see how and why other teachers have begun to make the switch from basals to literature.

Chapter five: Listening—to yourself and the children—is at the heart of any
Listen to teach   language program. I have a hunch that listening is the most important of all the language areas. But when learning is primarily teacher directed and language concepts are broken down into meaningless units, both teachers and children find it difficult to listen to themselves or to each other. Chapter 5 includes Actions to encourage you to begin to listen to yourself during your own reading and writing as a prelude to learning to listen to the children in your classroom.

Chapter six: You will enjoy observing yourself learn. One good way to use
Experiment   literate occasions is to write about something you've recently
with learning   learned in order to find out *how* you learn. Chapter 6 provides Actions that encourage you to examine your own learning history and to experiment with your own learning. In the process you will also learn from others, help them to understand how you learn, and even teach them something new.

MAKING DECISIONS   In choosing an Action, start with your strengths. If you are
ABOUT ACTIONS   more comfortable with reading, start there. Get used to the rhythm of the Actions, and the routines that go with them, in those areas where you feel most at home.

     The major aim of this book is to help you make decisions about your own literacy and only then to recommend literacy activities for your classroom. Some of the Actions you try yourself you may eventually want to try with children, but in each instance, your experience should be your primary concern. In other words, start with your own literacy, then look at literacy in your classroom.

     Most of our preparation as professionals has been based on the assumption that we are all readers and writers and that reading and writing are an essential part of our lives. After all, we've been to college, and many have advanced degrees. But so much of the literacy we experienced in college and graduate school is of a secondary nature; that is, we studied the thoughts and ideas of others—*for* others. Of course, understanding the wisdom of the ages and acquiring basic knowledge about the world in science, mathematics, and social studies are important.

What is often missing, however, is a sense of ourselves as independent learners in those fields, as individuals with our own independent ideas based on our perception of specific information. We were not helped to see that reading, writing, speaking, and listening are essential tools. I suspect now that many of my college professors may have tried to help me become more independent, but at the time I simply wasn't ready. So much came my way in my courses that the mere fulfilling of assignments was a full-time activity. I barely kept my head above water. Many of you may have had a similar experience.

DON'T TAKE THE
JOURNEY ALONE

The best way to begin experimenting with the Actions is to try them with another teacher. You need not both be working on the same Action; in fact, your interests and strengths may be quite different. On the other hand, some of you may realize that your needs and those of a colleague are quite close and that mutual learning is important to you. You may both want to work on the same Actions at the start. The key is to have a friend with whom you can share precise descriptions of what you are doing so that you can gain practice in discovering how you learn best.

FINAL REFLECTION

This book is for you. Using it as your guide, you will rediscover your own literacy and, in doing so, enrich your life. You will listen to your own questions about your family, your community, and the world you live in. You will wonder about your perceptions of daily events. You will write regularly to understand what you see and to absorb the meaning of the information that emerges on your pages. You will read the work of others, "composing your own text" as you read. Your thoughts will interweave with those of others as you listen to the voices of professional authors and the writers in your classroom.

Children need to be part of a classroom in which the teacher makes literacy decisions. In this way they become "literacy apprentices" and find out for themselves what it means to make their own, independent literacy decisions.

As you become involved in experimenting with the Actions, you will be aware that you are making decisions. Remember that the decision to become engaged with your own literacy means that you will be saying "no" to something else. By concentrating for a significant period of time on various aspects of literacy, teaching, and learning, you will be able to maintain the commitment you need to acquire the proficiency you want for yourself—and for children. Work at each Action until you are comfortable enough to decide which one you want to try next.

3

write with children

Teachers like Nancie Atwell, Mary Ann Wessells, and Linda Rief have convinced me that, to encourage literacy among children, attention to teachers' literacy has to come first. The children in their classrooms went beyond the usual kinds of writing that accumulate in writing folders to write about challenging material because they asked big questions of themselves. Moreover, these same teachers saw their personal and professional lives change because they changed their own reading and writing patterns.

Once I had realized that teachers' literacy is primary, I ran into a classic case of writer's block. I couldn't figure out a way to help teachers write within the framework of their very busy lives. Teachers seemed to feel that to see themselves as writers they would have to write articles for publication or extensive, highly polished pieces. With such high expectations, few of them wrote at all: "It just can't be done. Maybe someday I will—when I retire."

I decided to experiment on myself. I live a busy life, not as busy as many teachers, but varied enough: on the road, in class, conducting research, performing administrative duties, and so on. I decided to see the effect of ten minutes of writing. In the past, when I encountered writer's block I'd say, "Well, I'll just write ten minutes worth of junk on that." Once I'd committed myself to junk, I'd say, "Well, let's fool with the junk or at least do a fair amount of detailed junk." As soon as I did that, I would be free of the block and having fun. This new experiment with what I have come to call "literate occasions" meant that I'd spot something during the day worth writing about for ten minutes, and in the evening or early the next morning I'd write in my spiral notebook. Of course I couldn't complete every piece in ten minutes. I might finish a few in five, but I found that I returned to many pieces because they were just beginning to develop when the ten minutes were up. That kind of writing, writing that is going somewhere, writing in which I'm discovering something, makes its own time. The hard part is finding those first ten minutes.

The experiment worked. Not only did I find a way to help teachers, but best of all, I found a way to change my own writing—and my whole approach to living.

ACTION: TAKE ADVANTAGE OF LITERATE OCCASIONS.

Our days are filled with occasions we could write about, especially if we wonder why they occur. This morning I got up at five-thirty and started my usual writing routine. I have discovered that I need a routine to get me going or I'd never get anything accomplished. Part of my routine began the night before: I set the timer on the coffee and laid out clean clothes. Now the dog wants to go out, the *Boston Globe* waits in its receptacle over the mail box, and the radio sits until I turn it on to hear the weather. Daily routines.

I started the last paragraph to show how I spot literate occasions in the midst of familiar routines and ended up doing a quick paragraph about how I start my day. When I put words on the page, I explore. Scenes and small details trigger larger scenes and important questions. That's the exciting part about writing.

Back to literate occasions. So far this morning I've spotted several. Most are inspired by the questions "Why?" or "How come?" For example, not long ago, my dog, Sadie, came into my study, looked me in the eye, and shivered; I thought she had a fever. "Betty, what's wrong with the dog?" I shouted to my wife in the next room. "Oh, I'm blowing up balloons for the birthday party and every once in a while one pops." That was enough. In that incident there was a whole history of Sadie's fear of guns, thunder, anything that goes boom. If I were to write about that occasion, I'd take ten minutes, start with Sadie's trembling, think of her past reactions to loud sounds, and even speculate about other dogs (maybe some like loud sounds if they hunt).

Here are some more literate occasions: I tap the barometer; it drops a whole point, and I think about hurricanes, especially hurricane Carol, which swept through when I was in the Coast Guard. This is the month of September, and I can remember my first hurricane—in 1938. I look outside and spot my large thermometer, which is mounted on a tree; I paid good money for it, but it doesn't work. Every time I look at it I get angry. Maybe if I write about it I'll find out why I'm angry and possibly why I'm fascinated with the weather. (Why don't I take the thermometer down? Do I want to stay angry?)

Life presents us with edges, questions, moments, and experiences to listen to and observe. I only have to pick up the morning newspaper and hundreds of these occasions leap off the page, things that make me laugh or produce anger. At the same time, there are whole pages I don't understand, like the stock market reports. And I never look at advertisements (why don't I?). When I write for ten minutes I take the questions, joys, and complexities of life and set them down in front of me on the page so that I can see them, and maybe understand them a little better.

Too much of my life is spent in routine activities: get up, shave, dress, stagger down for my cup of coffee, write, eat, write some more, pile up my correspondence and teaching necessities in my canvas L. L. Bean bag, drive unseeing to work, wonder about where I might be lucky enough to find a parking spot, walk into the office to check phone calls and correspondence. . . . If someone were to ask me to write about my day at this point I would be forced to say, "What day?" There hasn't been anything new to it yet, no whys, just a kind of survival, like wading through a marsh. Sometimes I have whole days like that, or a string of days with the edges of living knocked off. If someone were to suggest that I write about those days, I might have two reactions: nothing happened so why bother, or it was too painful to revisit: "I'd just as soon forget it."

But literate people don't want to forget anything—pain, sadness, joy, anger. They want to tell stories about these experiences to themselves and to friends, to write about them in a diary, a journal, or a short essay. Writing allows us to look at an experience from two angles: at the moment it occurs and at the moment we write about it.

GETTING STARTED   Start with a commitment to ten minutes of writing and then decide on your own best time for doing it. We all have different biorhythms. I'm a morning person; I go downhill after 9:00 A.M. You may be a late night or a late morning person. I also find it helpful to "piggyback" writing onto already established routines. I make coffee, leave the kitchen—and sit down to write. Or, since I always watch the evening news, I sometimes go directly from the news to my study. Or, just after the children go out the door in the morning to catch the bus, or go to bed, or if I have ten minutes alone at the end of the school day, I write . . . or I may write for ten minutes when the students sit down to write.

Once you have set a time, the next questions are what and how you will write. Here are a few guidelines:

1. Write about what you know.
2. Write with details; sketch rapidly.
3. Don't revise in early drafts.
4. Experiment, but be yourself.

As Donald Murray says, "You can't write about nothing." But most of us have had that exact experience in school: we were asked to write about topics that "everyone" ought to be able to write about. Well, I can't choose topics for you, but I can show you where some topics have come from in my own life. They usually begin with wonder or a question . . . an itch that needs scratching. Some topics I've already mentioned, like my dog, Sadie. I'll write for five minutes now about that one. I'll simply start at the beginning and write a rough sketch:

I leaned into my computer, hunched over, pushed at some words, when I felt a presence to my right. The presence was slightly below my right elbow. The presence made a huffing sound and I looked. My dog Sadie, eyes slightly bulging and glazed, licking her lips and with trembles that shuddered, starting at her shoulders and working their way to her tail, only to begin again at the shoulders, seemed to be dumping on me. "What's the matter Sadie?" I asked, as if the dog could answer. She did, with a slight whimper.

"What's the matter with the dog?" I yelled to my wife in the other room, not really expecting an answer. "I'm blowing up balloons for the party tonight and one of them just broke." "Ah," I thought, "same old deal. Gunshots, or anything resembling them, set her off. But why does she plead with me? What does she expect me to do? Hold her, make them go away? I wonder.

That was five minutes of writing, five minutes of experimenting with words, trying to match words and images. Several times I did an instant replay of Sadie's face in my mind as I composed a sentence, each phrase setting off another replay from the beginning:

- Eyes bulging.
- Glazed eyes.
- Licking lips.
- Trembles—what the nature of?
- Shoulders to tail.
- Rhythm of shaking.
- Back to start again.

Many of the words lack precision (*glaze*) and do not convey the nature of her shaking, the rhythm of her trembling, and other images of what went on. But that doesn't bother me. Questions like those usually remain after a quick draft. Notice that I didn't say the dog was frightened—I didn't really know if she was frightened or sick or both. What I tried to do was to show the dog—to myself first, then to the reader. I didn't prejudge the event: "Oh, she's frightened." I've been fooled too many times. Now I know that I must first present the details to myself and then see where those details lead me. And, if I do a good enough job with the details, the reader, who may be more experienced with dogs, will say, "I have a better conclusion than yours," or perhaps, "I've seen dogs shake and that isn't the way they shake."

Writing routines are essential for any kind of personal breakthrough in literacy. There is a common notion that writers feel inspired and then they write. But it is just the opposite. They write (sometimes not knowing if anything will happen), and then *maybe* they will be inspired. In my writing routine I write the best junk I know how to write, or I might lower my standards just to get something on the page that will tell me, "No, it isn't that . . . it's that other thing over there, something I see out of the corner of my eye, something lurking in the back of my head."

Writing is learning to listen to yourself and your own voice, to watch for the sense of self that emerges, and to trust what you see coming. That's what will give you the courage to question the world, to compare your evidence with the evidence presented by others. The key here is that since you already have your evidence, you can seek to learn from the evidence of others. That kind of learning is just plain fun.

Here are a few lines from another, very different piece. I wrote this one last night in about fifteen minutes, getting a little silly in the process and having fun.

When I first stand in line to go through Customs I feel a dull, funny feeling creep up to my stomach, sort of like the time I could see on my mother's face that she knew I was lying about feeling sick and not being able to go to school. It's the same kind of guilt, only with Customs I haven't done anything, but it is a little like facing your mother on a bad day.

I'd always wondered why I felt a crazy sort of guilt before going through Customs. I wrote to find out and ended up realizing that the feeling was the same as when I was a boy.

I spotted another writing occasion when I was standing in line at McDonald's yesterday. I noticed a couple in front of me who were standing at the counter waiting for service. Now I'll sketch in a few lines to find out what was there:

An elderly couple, elbows resting on the busy McDonald's counter, stood next to each other waiting for service. The woman, wearing a plain print dress on a blue, autumn day in North Conway, New Hampshire, was about forty pounds overweight and uncertain of her place at the counter. She mumbled to her husband on the right, tossing her head in his direction when she did so. He, also overweight, stared ahead, as if not hearing her words. She looked down the long counter at the other cash registers and lines of people as if to study how the service worked at McDonald's. I moved over behind them but directly in front of the cash register, figuring I'd come after them but would be seen by the McDonald's counter worker. The woman, taking in my move, moved her ample hip in front of the register, and barked an order to the girl behind the counter.

When I began to write about it, I had only a fuzzy memory of yesterday's quick stop at McDonald's. But the woman— clothes, bulk, and all—emerged on the page as I wrote, and I recalled my embarrassment, wondering if she thought I was trying to get waited on ahead of her. At McDonald's I didn't know I would write about that woman today, but this morning I realized that the itch had to be scratched, so I wrote.

I must confess that when I wrote this one, I didn't follow my own advice. I had trouble remembering what the woman looked like and how she stood at the counter. Sensing that the work would be worth the effort, I wrote and rewrote until I could see her before I proceeded with the rest of the piece. Maybe I just wanted to *see* her again rather than to understand what happened at the counter. You'll find that, as you become more aware of yourself as a writer, you'll do what you sense is right when your information leads you to try a different process.

This next piece was the result of my experience in teaching my first university class of the year. A number of mix-ups in rooms, attendance, and so on ripped a hole in my well-made plans for that first class. I got rattled because I was behind, and because I was behind and knew things weren't going well, I said to myself, "I'll write about this to see what happened." I dedicated ten minutes to writing about the class. I had a hunch that ten minutes was too little time to really get into such a complex subject, so I tried to describe one moment in the two-and-a-half-hour session and then looked at the whole event through the smaller one, something I do quite often with complex issues.

I asked the class to share something that had happened to them. We sat in a large circle, a circle used to twenty people, but there were only fifteen of us in a very large room, and too far apart, so that sharing became more of an address to a large room and to strangers than a close-in sharing to an intimate session. Last year and in the spring people met in my study, a carpeted, book-filled room with sweeping counters and restful furniture. I could feel the students' words hanging in the air with little group response; the atmosphere was false, forced, a few chuckles here and there, but no real belly laughs like I usually hear when people are comfortable with each other, even in first sessions.

I looked across the room, noting the gaps in the chairs and the slight, nervous features of the students. I could feel the tension in my own body, a need to do something dramatic, some ninth inning grand slam with the bases loaded, to pull things out. Instead, I just said, "Time for a break. Let's be back together in ten minutes."

That occasion didn't work for me. I wanted to show what the group was like, but the details wouldn't come. I needed to show a student, and the student's own uneasiness. I suspect that the details are there, but I couldn't quite bring myself to see them. Maybe the experience was too painful. As I read over the sentences, I note all kinds of coaching on my part, because I can't trust the reader with the meager details that *are* there. "Nervous features of the students": but I didn't show their nervous features so that we could decide for ourselves if they were nervous. "The atmosphere was false": another conclusion without evidence. If I'd included more details about the room, we would have been able to draw our own conclusions about the atmosphere. But I'm not upset. I tried an experiment and it didn't work, but now I know what I might do if I took another crack at it. And I learned something: I tend to avoid details in considering complex, emotional issues. When things are "out there," like the lady at McDonald's or my dog, I write better. But when my own ego is at stake, I circle the subject because the subject is me. I'm in the center, blocking the reader. How can I get around this obstructive self? By first describing in detail what is *outside*. As I sit "out there" among the details, I can look back at the words on the page and through them know what I think and feel. Then I can make more artful selections in subsequent drafts.

Here's an occasion that may lead to an article. A week and a half ago, our University of New Hampshire research team started a new study in Stratham, New Hampshire, about children's growing ability to evaluate their own work. I decided to write about my first hour in the school, starting from the parking lot. Since the data about the outside of the school were written down rather quickly and in first draft, they closely resemble writing occasions. Here is what I wrote:

As I looked at the outside of the school on the cloudy day with the east wind gusting at the school flag and a promise of rain from the slight mist, I thought, "Wonder if there will be outside recess this morning. Teachers and children need outdoor recess on the first day—any day for that matter." I walked up the long walk on the north side of the school, noting the landscaping and begonias among the woodchips. "Good aesthetics." I opened the door, heard no sound. I suppose I expected to hear the sound and bustle on the first day.

I paused to admire again the Chagall-like panels done by the children the spring before. Three panels to the left and three straight ahead from floor to ceiling, with bright reds, yellows, and greens, favorites of the children, and their voices that rose in canted perspectives and exaggerated sizes. "What a tone for a school," I thought, "a great mood setter for anyone entering or visiting a school."

I would like to do an article on school entrances and the messages visitors—and especially parents, teachers, and children—receive during the walk to the school door and in the first fifteen or twenty feet inside the building. If a lead is important in an article, the message people receive in the "lead statement" in a school is equally important. My point here is that literate occasions come out of other occasions. Pieces are embedded in other pieces. I could write about the approach to the school, the entryway, and the first corridor from the viewpoint of a parent, a child, a teacher, or an administrator and get four different pieces.

Shirley Weitzel, a school principal in Stratford, Ontario, takes advantage of literate occasions. In the following example, she wrote about a dog waiting outside the library by asking a simple question: "I wonder what the story is about this waiting dog?" She took down some notes about what she saw and, later, she wrote for ten minutes.

THE DOG AND I

As I walked along the tree-lined path leading to the library, I spied the black statue of a dog sitting on the step. His jet black hair was groomed and clean. Although it was raining, only the top of his head was wet as if he had been standing under a dripping tap. The blue bandana with white polka dots was carefully tied around his neck. Like a stone, he sat on his haunches staring straight ahead. The ear twitching, the tail wagging, the head revolving with each click of the library door. He bothers no one. Patiently waiting for his master to emerge. Stretching his paws in front of him he lies down, growing tired of his vigil. Restless now, he stands, slowly walking toward the door, seeking shelter under the canopy. Searching with his nose pressed against the cement he traces a familiar scent. Maintaining a safe distance from the automatic door he settles, content to begin the vigil again.

The lady in the cream-colored suit and beige high heels stops as she exits from the library. Looking down, she smiles, and greets the dog. "Hi there." Ignored, she opens her multi-colored umbrella and continues on her way.

Together we wait, the dog and I, for the master. My anticipation begins to match his. As though synchronized, our heads turn with each click of the latch. Time, who is my master, calls and I obey. I turn to leave and marvel at the patience of my canine friend. Although I did not meet his master I know he is not . . . [end of ten minutes].

Lois Connors, an eighth-grade teacher in Hudson, New Hampshire, wrote a piece that wasn't triggered by an experience but by the notion that books have always been special to her. She wrote to understand what books mean to her.

I love books. I don't just love to read them. I like to hold them, run my fingers lightly over the covers, the pages, the pictures. I like to dream the stories waiting between the covers. I even like to smell books . . . especially old books, books from my childhood, those given to me by people all but forgotten but for the book they left . . . I am delighted when some tiny trace of a previous reader is evident in the pages: a turned page, the petal of a rose, a cookie crumb, a slip of a bookmark, or best of all a name inside the cover.

At once, in all of those occasions, I have companionship with another reader. I especially love children's books. I have not yet (and know I never shall) grown too old for beautiful pictures, fine line sketches, big bold pages. I loved Make Way for Ducklings . . . *that may be the first book I truly remember being in love with. I used to hold my breath and all but burst with excitement when once each spring, just before Easter, we would go into Boston to the Common. I would hope to catch a glimpse of the Mallard family crossing the street. I never did. But most of all, I love to buy books. I confess. I have bought more books than I can keep up with reading though no matter how many I buy, it's never as many as I'd like. I don't have a particular favorite bookstore. Any place will do. I've been on this campus for only two weeks and I think I have made nine trips into the bookstore. True, I was in search of* Billy the Kid *for a while, but when I couldn't manage to nail him down, I decided on* The Education of a Yankee. *Then there was* Frederick *staring from the shelf in the children's section. I remember how he gathered the sun's rays and colors to keep warm in winter, and I had to replace the copy I could no longer find. Marge Piercy . . . both Don and Tom read poems of hers to us. I think I'll pick this one up. And so the ten-minute browse through Barnes and Noble goes on rainy lunch hours. Day by day, I think just one more book. I'll only be here a few more days. Day by day my list of recommended books grows. Just when I thought it was safe to go into a bookstore, I came to Durham.*

In this first draft, Lois showed herself the details of her love for books by following the thoughts triggered by her memory. In her draft we meet a book lover, and stories of our own book memories come to life. Lois didn't worry about sentence structure or paragraphing, she just wrote, expressing a freshness of observation that she has come to trust through her writing.

THE INVESTMENT NEEDED

After two years of working with literate occasions, both for myself and with other teachers, I find that a daily investment of about twenty minutes, or the writing of two ten-minute pieces every day, for two weeks, will be enough to launch you as a writer. You will begin to see differently and be sensitive to incidents you hadn't known were there. Best of all, writing will become a part of you.

Ten minutes will give you a new way of looking at the world. After a while your writing may not stop after ten minutes. I find that I return to many pieces, which later become poems or short fiction or just keep on going into extensive articles or sketches that run for pages. Some of these I share; many I don't. They are for me first; then I'll decide if I want others to see them.

MAKE IT WORK   The most difficult thing about writing is getting there. It is no more difficult to *get* to paper and pencil, typewriter, or computer for ten minutes than it is to work on writing a book for two hours. Writing about literate occasions is unassigned writing; the question is, how can you reach the point where you discover enough about the power of writing for yourself to look forward to returning to it?

Discovering the power of writing requires daily writing. Most of my writer friends have a small sign in their study that says *"Nulla dies sine linea"* (No day without a line). This advice not only contributes to the quality of the writing, it makes writing so much easier. Every day missed makes it doubly difficult to get back to it. It takes time for the mind to reengage itself with the notion of writing, to say nothing of picking up on those ideas and thoughts that were brewing during the lost day.

Keep lists   "Heavens," you might say to yourself, "I can't come up with so many different occasions to write about. I'll run out of topics and I'll know my life for what it is: boring." Once again, turn back to observing and listening. Look at what makes you angry or joyful and discover the details behind it. Keep lists of those feelings and what causes them, but when you write, don't mention the feeling itself. Instead, play with words.

Be playful Most of us have been taught that "writing is a serious business." It is. And because it is serious, it requires some playfulness. Remember my anger about the thermometer that didn't work? Well, yesterday I took it down. Here is what I came up with in a rough ten-minute write:

> *My large outdoor thermometer has stared at me for four months now without working. The arrow has remained on 68 degrees on a hot August day, or a cool September morning when I'd guess the temperature at 42 degrees.*
>
> *My writing made me take it down. That's right. I finally walked over and took it off the tree where it is mounted. I'd see how imperfect the designers had made that expensive thermometer.*
>
> *It wasn't the designers' fault. It was probably mine. On the back plate of the white, plastic thermometer are four holes about a quarter inch in width, probably air holes to let air in to make the thin metal strip expand or contract and control the arrow that records the temperature. Since I had placed the thermometer against the tree, earwigs discovered holes for a nest and took up lodging on the inside of the plate. I counted six earwigs, which poked their heads out of the holes like woodchucks in June. I took the thermometer inside to place it underwater to make the rest of the earwigs come out. I'll admit I was a little angry at the little rascals and I'd disturb their pleasant quarters with a bath. They kept coming out. I'd guess about twelve to thirteen earwigs came out of that three-inch-wide housing. I can't get at the gunk from eggs or refuse they've put in there and will have to buy another thermometer.*

That was an eight-minute exercise. It was fun discovering again my own surprise at the cause of the thermometer's malfunction, and I enjoyed sketching in the details, sharpening my mind's eye. I especially enjoy sharing this bit of trivia with you.

ACTION: FIND SOME READERS.

One of the barriers to writing can be the question "Write for what?" I write mostly for myself, but I'd be a liar if I said I didn't enjoy sharing these small episodes with you. Who is the "you"? Although my ultimate audience is you, the many readers across the country, I can't wait for you to respond. I'll show this chapter to the people closest to me, my wife, Betty, and my colleagues Jane Hansen and Don Murray, or tuck it in the mail to my friend and fellow writer, Nancie Atwell in Boothbay Harbor, Maine.

Start your work on these Actions by working with a friend. The ideal is to have your friend agree to enter into the discipline of writing about literate occasions with you. Share your work, talk about your writing over the phone. If you are teachers, share at break or in the teachers' room. I'd suggest sharing in a specific way: Read your piece aloud to hear your own voice or give it to your friend to read and ask, "What strikes you in this? What do you think this is about? What do you remember?" Ask your friend to please keep to these questions because you don't want a critique at this point; what you need to know is what *came through*, what the reader *understood*. Questions and suggestions can come later—and on other pieces.

HOW TO HANDLE   The most common cause of writer's block is setting standards
WRITER'S BLOCK   that are too high. Perhaps you have been trying to impress someone with your writing, or you've been using extra adjectives or adverbs to sound "literary," as you were taught to do in junior high school English. Writers write in simple, direct language and try to sound like themselves. Lower your stan-

dards a little when you feel blocked and start putting down words, any words.

When I feel blocked I write short, complaining pieces. I write about not being able to write. Once again, words on the page and a mind in motion will help you write yourself out of writer's block.

WHY WRITE? The very stance teachers take toward the world through personal learning and inquiry, the "why" questions they trigger because they wonder about the world are the strongest contributors to the literate climate of their classrooms. I wrote about my thermometer thinking my piece would be about shoddy manufacturing and ended up with one that touched on biology. I wrote about my dog's fears and wondered why some dogs are terrified by loud noises and why others, trained to hunt, relish them.

Through it all, I continue to learn about myself, because I describe in detail the everyday issues around me and end up discovering my own point of view. I begin to acquire a voice and a sense of assurance about what I know of the world around me. The more I see and understand, the more I am free to wonder, to be struck by mystery, to express doubt. Writing is too important to be relegated only to children; it is important enough for us all to include as a basic part of our own lives.

read with children

Yesterday, when I walked through the library of Stratham Memorial School, where our University of New Hampshire research team is in the middle of a new research project, my colleague Jane Hansen hailed me. "Don, listen to this. You like Byrd Baylor, but listen to what she's written here in this book for children [*The Other Way to Listen*]. 'If you think you are better than the horned toad, you will never hear its voice.' Isn't that profound?"

I had to agree. If for one minute I think I am better than someone, I won't hear what that person has to say. At least three or four times a week Jane and I read some line, a few paragraphs, or sometimes several pages aloud to each other. Listening to books, listening to our own voices in dialogue, or debating with other authors is one of the joys of the literate life.

Books allow me to experience thousands of lives I can never lead. They allow me to crawl inside the thinking of adventurers, admirals, parents of suffering children, bank clerks, Russians, Indians, ballerinas, authors, and athletes. In the midst of my reading, I sometimes think of a friend who would enjoy the very passage or book I am reading, and as I continue to read my friend is at my shoulder, nodding and laughing or shaking her head at the text as it unfolds.

I'm not the reader I'd like to be. I'm envious of Jane's ability to tuck reading into the nooks and crannies of the day; yet when I find myself waiting for someone who is late for an appointment, I groan and moan, look at my watch, and fret through the delay. "Take out a book and read," Jane abruptly advised me one day. "No need to waste the time." She's right, of course.

Reading, like writing, requires some discipline if you aren't used to it. Most people don't read. A very small part of our population, about 3 percent, buys 95 percent of the books sold in bookstores, graphic evidence of the nonsuccess of our basal reading programs. The children in these programs do not become adult readers.

Basal reading programs also affect our own reading as teachers. As in many jobs and professions, we come to "resemble" the materials with which we work. The kind of literate engagement children have with a controlled sound/symbol, sight vocabulary book is very different from the kind of literate engagement they have with books by fine writers like Byrd Baylor, Ezra Jack Keats, A. J. Rey, and Beverly Cleary. Writers like these provide literate space for readers and a broad base for engagement and interpretation. They speak in unique voices and make important artistic choices. They engage children's minds differently. What we overlook is that teachers don't escape the type of thinking represented by basals, either. When children can share their reading of wonderful books, they encounter many minds: the teacher's, other children's, the author's, and their own. Each provides space for the thinking of others.

During workshops and even in major speeches I often ask those in the audience to take out a piece of paper and write down three books they've read in the last year, to turn to the person next to them, and to say a little about each one. The partners listen carefully, ask questions, and then reverse the procedure. I am always struck by several realizations during this brief, fifteen-minute interchange: many people discover new books and meet a new person in a unique way; books are great openers; others aren't readers and don't know what to say. The intent of this sharing is to emphasize what we can learn about people and books in a short time, but the underlying implication is that, obviously, this is what we in the profession do all the time.

Most school programs do not assume that teachers are readers—or expect them to be. Basal approaches do not make the teacher's own reading a part of the children's ongoing daily activity of learning to read. But as is true for the other aspects of literacy I will stress in this book, reading must begin with the teacher first. It must be a vital part of the teacher's necessary diet as a literate person, or little of signficance will happen for the children. Changing reading habits, encouraging a teacher's own involvement in reading, may be even more difficult than opening new doors in our own writing and in the writing of children.

FICTIONS ABOUT READING

There may be more fictions about reading than there are about writing, and these fictions keep us from reading. They make us wait for a day that never comes. We say to ourselves, "Some-day I'll get back to Shakespeare." Many of them are holdovers from the last college English class we had fifteen years ago or even current infections from the teaching of reading in our public schools. Here is a short list:

- College graduates ought to be reading the classics.
- Popular fiction is a cop-out to intellectual inquiry.
- Reading is not signficant unless you have to struggle with the text.
- Beware of reading for enjoyment.
- Children's books rarely contain important ideas for adults.
- Read in order to please other people; leave yourself out of the engagement.
- Teachers should only read journals and professional books.

Starting with our first days in school we have been condi-tioned to leave our own voices and our interpretations of texts at home. "What is the author saying?" "What does this mean?" From our first reading group in elementary school through our last graduate course, our teachers and professors have directed us in how to analyze the "text" of the author. They have already given us their interpretation of the text, and they want us to know it as precisely as they do. Make no mistake, the text is important, but the texts we create are also significant because they are the texts we live by. If we speak of the writer's voice, we also need to speak of the reader's voice. We read with a double awareness: this is what the author is saying; this is what I think.

Reading, like writing, must be for us first, and only then for the children in our classrooms. (Why should they have all the fun?) We need to rediscover the joy of reading, hear our own voices in the text, and learn again how reading can change our own engagement with the world. This chapter will provide two sets of Actions, reading for ourselves and reading for the children, which are intended to benefit both.

ACTION: START TO READ.

I write much more easily than I read, but it hasn't always been this way. In recent years I've simply had so much writing to do that it now comes more easily. I tuck reading in throughout the day, but I haven't found a good time to read the way I wish. And I feel so far behind in my reading that I don't read well. When I don't read well, my enjoyment drops, and when my enjoyment drops I avoid reading, even for pleasure. I need to think through my reentry into reading.

Book choices   People want to read for diverse reasons. Maybe you don't even know which books you'd start with. If so, start by reading different kinds of writing. Where possible, share them with other people. Here are a number of ways you might begin. Choose at least three of the following and read each one for ten or fifteen minutes.

- A newspaper editorial.
- The first two pages of a magazine article.
- A poem (read it aloud).
- The first two pages of a novel.
- The beginning of a children's book (a title one of your children might read).

- The first two pages of a book you own that you've wanted to read (it is sitting on the shelf waiting for you).
- The beginning of a "how-to" article about something you've always wanted to be able to do.
- A book you don't want anyone else to know you are reading.
- A challenging book you've always wanted to read.
- A book by an author you've wondered about.

Book reading The next day, go back and spend at least half an hour reading the one that interested you most, or choose three new selections.

Relaxed reading is unhurried reading, pure self-indulgence. You read what you wish, even skipping over parts that don't interest you. You're not trying to impress anyone, least of all yourself. You experiment and taste. You wonder about what strikes you.

Some of what strikes you may lead you to act. As the reading becomes yours, you say, "I think I'll do that." Three months ago, Yetta Goodman introduced me to Byrd Baylor's *I'm in Charge of Celebrations*, a lovely book for children. I have found that well-written children's literature governs my actions and decisions as much as some adult literature. In this case, Byrd Baylor describes the wonders of the desert through the eyes of a young person who sets herself up as her own authority on celebrations. As she experiences dust devils and rainbows, she records them on her own calendar for celebration. "What a marvelous idea," I thought to myself. Since then I've written down four celebrations on next year's calendar (after all, I'm in charge).

Reading and notions of power are closely interrelated. Reading is a part of my daily routine, not because I have to read but because I need to. After all, if I'm in charge of celebrations and if I have the major responsibility for determining my life's direction, then I need help. Beyond that, I'm very curious about how other people operate, especially those who seem in charge of their lives.

My writing voice, which I establish by writing about literate occasions, makes me want to see how others write. So I read short columns and episodes in the *New Yorker*, and I especially read Lewis Thomas, whose short, thousand- to fifteen-hundred-word pieces first appeared in the *New England Journal of Medicine* and are now collected in *The Medusa and the Snail* and *Lives of a Cell*. Simply, yet profoundly written, they cover everything from warts to punctuation to beavers and otters. Thomas writes with a sense of wonder, one of his favorite words.

Reading gives me the chance to experience wonder through the lives of others. I can cross oceans, participate in presidential campaigns, survive on a raft, cycle around the world, or travel back to the midnineteenth century and read the words of Jean-Henri Fabre as he records the habits of the digger wasp.

Some reading is pure vacation. I want to leave this planet, forget the day, forget tomorrow. If I want adventure, I can indulge in a John MacDonald mystery and travel with Travis McGee. I let the characters do the work; some of them I don't like, and I read more rapidly to get by them, slowing down to listen to those I enjoy. I might even buy a crazier book than usual—some red-covered glossy—as I charge through an airport, because I want less than thinking. I want to be a totally different, even disreputable character. Still, I might be embarrassed enough about my purchase to rip off the cover and slump in my seat, leaning toward the window. Revealing? It sure is.

Stop occasionally as you read to read parts you like aloud. In fact, make reading aloud, which will be an important Action in this chapter, a part of your personal reading routine. Or think of someone with whom you'd like to share read-aloud moments. Two weeks ago I heard the poet Donald Hall read from his collection of poems, *The Happy Man*. He had so much fun reading "Scenic View" and "Great Day in the Cow's House" that I raced out, bought the collection, shut myself in my study, and read them aloud to an admiring wall. I had an urge to act not unlike my need to shoot baskets when I see Larry Bird swish a three-pointer with five seconds left in a Boston Celtics game.

Ted Kooser is another one of my favorite read-aloud poets. I'm the agrarian sort, and my feet and mind are in the soil where I was raised. When I get depressed or feel just plain out of it, I read aloud, one poem after another. A year ago, during a particularly difficult time, I read three of Ted's books aloud nonstop. I've done the same with the Psalms. I enter fully into the moment when I read aloud, feeling the pain and joy of the lines.

More respectable scholars may say, "You read Kooser? Then you can't be serious about Donald Hall." I don't care. I don't care what the leading scholars may say, or my high school English teacher, or the chair of the English department who put me on probation in college. My reading is for me, and I intend to use it as I will. On the other hand, some of my reading will be tested, and it should be. Professional reading, interpretations of research I want to share with others, directions for constructing something, detailed procedures—all are types of reading that need discussion and reexamination. I have a group of friends with whom I share this reading and questioning. My wife, Betty, is particularly frank and challenging, and well-schooled in taking another point of view.

ACTION: SHARE YOUR READING WITH OTHERS.

Half the fun of reading is sharing what you've encountered with others. My sharing may be as general as "Betty, listen to this," and then I read her a few lines. It is a little like introducing two friends whom you know but who have not met each other. With most of the books I read I know someone I'll want to recommend them to within a few chapters. I'll tell the person,

"When I finish this, I'd like you to take a look at it and see what you think." It isn't at all like an assignment. You know the book and you know the person—two friends who ought to meet.

Readers know who their fellow readers are. If you are just beginning to hike on the reading trail again, try thinking of a friend who is a reader when you read. On second thought, don't think of anyone at all. Audiences may not emerge until you are well into a book, as they do when you write. As you get to know the author, or certain characters and lines, the person with whom you'll share will become clear. Just keep in mind the notion that you'll share something with someone before you finish the book.

The person you share with may be across the hall or several towns away, and a phone call will make the connection. On the other hand, a short letter or even a written response to the book you've just read will be enough to open the conversation. The critical element is that you are in control. The reading histories of many of us included no book sharing; if we shared anything, it was with the teacher—through a test or a book report, or in response to a question addressed to the class. But readers need to experiment with audiences; in the beginning these should be self-chosen.

ACTION: READ ALOUD TO CHILDREN.

The best place to begin sharing is with our own students. Reading aloud to children every day establishes one of the essential conditions for the literate classroom. Children meet different authors, get to know characters, and learn from plots through the medium of shared books. They acquire a common experience of literate events, which they can refer to in conversation or in writing. They become a literate community.

When I read aloud, I choose the books I like. Some serve the purpose better than others. Books like *Charlotte's Web* by E. B. White—or almost any of his books—transcend age boundaries. Ask the local school or town librarian to recommend books for reading aloud to your children. Then practice reading several of the recommended titles aloud to see which one interests you the most. If it interests you, and you feel your voice engaging more fully with that of the author, the children will enjoy it more.

Reading aloud takes practice. Once in a great while, I'll pick up a book and read it to the class without practicing, but most of the time I read a selection several times beforehand, especially if it is one I haven't previously read. For longer selections, especially books with chapter divisions, I practice on the first two chapters. By then, I usually feel the voice of the writer accurately enough to continue without practicing further. I know the writer and the characters, and I sense the direction of the book.

Voice is a word that usually needs explaining. When people speak or write, they have their own intonation, emphasis, way of selecting words, and personality, all of which mix with the storytelling. As you read, listen for the sound of the person in the words. Don't worry about matching your voice to the author's, because your interpretation and your voice will blend in. That's the way it has to be. Even if I don't read a selection to an audience, I often read portions aloud to myself just to listen to the author's voice. Listening to voices is nearly a full-time activity in a literate life. I listen for my own when I write and mine in tandem with others when they speak. I try on the voices of characters in fiction or poets in poetry. I get to know people by trying their voices on for size.

When I read aloud, I can usually tell if my reading is going well by the variety of voices I hear in my reading. My voice expresses meaning according to my sense of the author's unfolding purpose. As the meaning emerges, I hope my voice becomes consistent with my ongoing interpretation.

You may find it helpful to share an oral reading of one book with another person. Read it first yourself, then read it with someone and discuss the reasons for the different interpretations your voices have given to the text. You may find that you wish to keep your own interpretation, but you may also want to adopt your partner's. In either case, you will have a clearer understanding of your own use of voice as you read.

In summary, start with books that suit you. If you enjoy humor, choose books that allow you to laugh along with the children. Practice by reading aloud by yourself and try several different ways of approaching the meaning of a text. Plan to share an interpretation with a friend, even if you both read only a few paragraphs.

ACTION: LET CHILDREN READ.

There is a small revolution going on in the field of reading: children are reading "real" books. Nancie Atwell (1984) records what happened in her eighth-grade classroom in Boothbay Harbor, Maine.

Last year's eighth graders, including eight special education students, read an average of twenty-four full-length works, from Blume to Bronte to Verne to Vonnegut to Irving—Washington and John.

She describes the revolution more fully in her book *In the Middle*. Her approach was a simple one: let the children read in school and then write about and talk about books just as they did about their own writing. Make reading relevant by letting the students choose their own books, and relate them to daily living and to the big questions that arise in the lives of young adolescents who struggle with growing up. Above all, encourage them to share books with each other. Atwell wrote over two thousand letters to her students during the year, discussing ideas, extending their thinking—and recommending more books.

Nancie's approach was one of total immersion in literacy. Her class was immersed because she was constantly reading and writing herself. The line between writing and reading time was blurred. The relationship between teacher and student changed: they recommended books for her to read—and she read them. She used no set method. Rather, she established conditions in which literate events could occur. The time she had spent correcting papers she used instead to respond directly in writing to her students' thinking. The time she had spent telling the students about the literature they ought to know, she instead spent engaging a few students in conferences while the rest read. Her logic was simple: if the students read *in* school, they would read *out of* school. And they did, devouring books from nearby libraries and from bookstores in other towns.

Pat McLure and Leslie Funkhouser of Mast Way Elementary School in Lee, New Hampshire, have worked to establish conditions for reading in the primary years that are consistent with those for writing.* As in Atwell's classroom, there is no ability grouping for reading. Children of mixed ability levels meet to discuss their books and share their reading journals.

The entire faculty at Stratham Memorial School in Stratham, New Hampshire found out in three short months what happens when you let children read. Two teachers started, and one by one the other teachers joined them. Teachers had their own approaches to reading, but they did have one thing in common: they agreed that children should choose books and read in school. Stories about children's initiative and extended book reading, and discussions about better books for children to read, became the substance of talk in the teachers' room. The rapid shift from basals to trade books did not occur in a vacuum. It was a logical extension of these teachers' stance toward children's writing. Many revealed that they'd had an itch to do something about reading for some time; they knew their approaches were inconsistent but didn't know what to replace them with. Most were surprised at the simplicity of the change.

---

* Leslie Funkhouser now teaches second grade at an elementary school in Virginia.

Fourth-grade teacher Paula Walsh told about her first day with her new approach to reading:

PAULA: I told them I was going to have books from the library, town, and school, as well as the classroom library and any books of their own they wanted to bring in. We were going to use these to read from. I explained how we'd start the morning. I explained the three types of books (the children were to try a variety described as easy, medium, and difficult) and the logs to keep track of the reading and how we'd write about how we felt about our reading.

And then we started. I just wanted them to begin without any rules and guidelines. I wanted to know how it would go first. As days went by we began to talk more about what they needed to know, what I was looking for, and the process of going about reading and getting books, sharing and writing. The amazing thing was they took to it very easily. Maybe it was writing process or the fact that they really liked this way of doing reading. It kind of flowed. It was incredible how much they read and how quiet it was. So I really didn't get into the structure of it until later, at least not verbally with them. I wanted them to experience it before I made decisions about it.

I want to stress that Paula's transition was a natural shift because of what she was already doing in her teaching of writing. The children were used to sharing, receiving, and questioning their own texts in writing. They were used to listening to each other and taking responsibility for their learning. Many of these procedures have already been outlined in *Writing: Teachers & Children at Work* (Graves 1983). The shift from texts written by student authors to those written by trade authors was not as great as it may first appear.

For years basals have held children back from reading. Basals are geared far more to teachers than to children, to a population of nonreading "professionals" who have become trapped by manuals and exercises. The children spend one week on five pages of basal text and extensive workbook exercises, and respond to questions that couldn't possibly make real connections with their own lives. Even worse, there is no provision for the questions that children might initiate *about their own reading,* the most important questions in any learner's profile. Basals are designed to deal with children's weaknesses rather than their strengths. Under these circumstances, each year there is less and less incentive for children to read on their own. Each basal is carefully structured to help children get ready for the *next* basal, when in fact, basals were originally created to free children to read trade books.

When a school system makes a million-dollar investment in basals, workbooks and manuals, and reading personnel, how can it let children be free to read? When will we let children use the major part of classroom reading time to do what helps them most: read?

We worry about the standardized tests; these tests have created their own kind of prison. It is now possible to go from first grade through the Graduate Record Examination and never read more than a few paragraphs at a time to answer four to five questions in the reading selection. Basal reading materials follow the tests in order to guarantee better scores. They have come to resemble the tests: short paragraphs of sterile information written with little individual voice and little provision for the reader's own space or interests are intended to assess the student's ability to read. Thank heaven we don't assess people's eating abilities in the same way. If we did, we'd test people's ability to consume tablespoons of crumbs and wonder all the while about their lack of interest in eating "real food." Worse, we, the examiners, wouldn't even know a good meal if we saw one. So we would continue to wonder about the nuances of good and bad crumbs.

What to do on day one Prepare by helping children have books to read. Announce, as Paula Walsh did, that they will need to bring books of their own choosing to class from the classroom library, school and town libraries, home, friends, anywhere. At first it may not seem as if there are enough books to go around, but when children begin to read each day in school, not only does their reading improve, their ability to find books they want to read does also. I have not yet encountered a school or a classroom in which books could not be provided when children were demanding to read them. We forget how underused most libraries are. We, with the children, will find the books. It is an exciting game to play.

Let the children read without interruption for a good block of time on the first day—a minimum of twenty to twenty-five minutes. If they are just starting their books, they'll need a good stretch to break into the text. Read with them.

At the end of the reading time, gather everyone together in one place to share what they are finding in their books. Share your own: "This is what my book is about and this is what strikes me." Finally, introduce two or three new books by reading several passages aloud. Speculate on the outcomes of the books. This kind of oral sharing of books is the backbone of a strong reading program. Children constantly introduce authors, characters, plots, and favorite passages to each other, both orally and in writing.

Succeeding days There are a number of systems that can be used for choosing books. Paula used the system employed by Leslie Funkhouser. Children have three books in their possession at any one time of easy, medium, and challenging levels of difficulty. It is important for children, and for all of us, to read easier books. A well-written easy book helps readers to take in ideas more readily and do some thinking they might not ordinarily do. Byrd Baylor's books do that for me. Some children's books in science and social studies choose and describe elementary concepts so well, they become sources of major learning. The medium book is roughly where the child finds it most comfortable to read. The challenging book is just that: it is a book above the child's reading level, yet a book that contains concepts or a story the child wants to pursue.

I used to worry, a throwback to my reading clinic days, that children would become frustrated if a book was above their "level." But when children choose their own books, the word "frustration" takes on a different meaning. They are seldom frustrated because they know that the teacher isn't waiting for a perfect performance on words they can't read. On occasion, when children become upset if some nuance of meaning is lost to them because they can't read certain words, they can consult other children or the teacher for help.

Some children don't choose a good balance in their reading. A few may read only difficult books; in that case, the teacher tells the child, "This week I'll choose a book I think is more in your range. You choose the other two books." The same approach is used when children read only easy books; if the problem persists, the teacher enters into the choice scheme for that week.

ACTION: ABOLISH READING GROUPS.

This Action—abolishing reading groups—may be as tough a decision as you will ever make in your teaching career. For most of my professional life I have conducted and recommended homogenous reading groups—the usual three levels. Abolishing reading groups is a tough social and political decision.

Throughout a decade of work with the writing process we never grouped children by ability levels. There simply was no need to. Because so little writing was taught, there was no tradition requiring writing groups. Our decision was easy. We hardly gave it a thought.

I recall so well the day Pat McLure, a first-grade teacher at

Mast Way Elementary School in Lee, New Hampshire, decided to abolish her reading groups. Pat had six reading groups at that time, with one child making up the sixth group all by himself. Because she had worked with ungrouped children in writing for two years, the illogical nature of grouping for reading became more and more apparent to her. Finally, Pat said to Ruth Hubbard, a researcher in her classroom, "Ruth, will you just scramble those reading groups; mix all the names up." Ruth began to move the name tags, which hung from cup hooks on a large board at the side of the room. A cluster of children quickly surrounded her. What Ruth and Pat heard from the children made them remark later, "We'll never go back to the old way of grouping." Two girls stood side by side, and one remarked to the other, "We don't really like this, do we?" The girls were in the top group and wondered about the reshuffling of the social order of the classroom. A boy, the one who was in the sixth group by himself, said, "Wow, I get to be with other kids."

When children read extensively in trade books, get help with skills in workshop sessions, and meet regularly with other children to discuss books, their perceptions of themselves as readers and the quality of their work change dramatically. I wonder why it has taken us so long to make the shift. Paula Walsh, a fourth-grade teacher at Stratham Memorial School, observes:

PAULA: That's what's so incredible about it. There is no high or low reader. There are no levels. There is a wide span of reading ability. It is not obvious any more like it was with reading groups. Children don't say, "We're the highest; we're the lowest." Everyone is reading what they can read. That to me is the biggest plus. My low readers enjoy it. They are not feeling any . . . they don't feel like they are placed at the low end of the spectrum; they read what they can read and do well at it. No one is zeroing in on what level of reading an individual is doing. And I really see where my low readers are having much more success. It is improving their whole self-concept. That's the biggest plus, along with the fact that everyone is reading.

I asked Paula what she meant by self-concept.

PAULA: A willingness to get up in front of the whole group, read from their book, tell about the book they are reading. That shows in both large and small group sharing, the confidence they have to sit with someone and recommend the book they have read. Their attitude at reading time is more positive. It is more relaxed. Before, they'd try to blend in with the woodwork more. They certainly didn't want to read in front of the others. And now they volunteer.

ACTION: HELP CHILDREN KEEP READING JOURNALS AND WRITE LETTERS ABOUT THEIR BOOKS.

Children talk about their books in the same way they talk about their writing. Both, after all, were composed by writers the children know as authors. They read as writers. Jane Hansen has written an extensive account of this in her book, *When Writers Read* (1987).

When teachers switched from basals with workbooks to trade book reading they felt the need to have some accountable way of showing children's thinking about their reading. They began by using journals. At first, children wrote accounts of what struck them in their reading, which resembled the familiar book report. The language in these accounts was stilted, with an impersonal, "to-whom-it-may-concern" tone. The writing was brief, repetitive, and uninteresting. The children enjoyed their reading but disliked the accounting required in the journal. Teachers enjoyed the uninteresting accounts even less.

Two years later, these journals contain a collection of letters about books and issues related to books. The letters go back and forth between child and teacher and, in some instances, between child and child. Nancie Atwell demonstrates this approach in her book *In the Middle*, when she describes how she writes letters to her students.

The following letters illustrate how one letter becomes a springboard for the next. When I look through one of these collections of letters, I find that some dialogues about a single subject last as long as three weeks and, in some instances, as little as two days. The selection presented here is from the second, third, fourth, and sixth grades at Stratham Memorial School.

In the first letter exchange (Figure 4–1), between Jared and Catherine Wansart, a second-grade teacher, Jared describes how he and his mother pretend to be the bunnies in the story. In response, Mrs. Wansart shares her experience of reading the book to her own children at home. As in many of her letters, she ends with a question, which Jared will answer in his next letter.

By third grade the exchange is more sophisticated (see Figure 4–2). Janis Bailey's letter to Lauren includes a brief reference to Lauren's discussion group and then moves on to the issue of why Lauren abandoned *Harriet the Spy*. Some of the most fruitful journal exchanges occur when students abandon certain books, a necessary part of learning to read independently. The letters written by both children and teachers in these journals is "first draft" writing. But make no mistake, in these classrooms children make many of their pieces as polished as they can.

Many of the questions teachers ask the children relate to their own lives. That is, teachers want to know children's reactions to what the characters in their stories are doing. In Figure 4–3 Nancy Herdecker, a fourth-grade teacher, asks Chris how people might be influenced by the book.

In Mrs. Herdecker's room, as in several others, the children classify the level of difficulty the book represents to them using

FIGURE 4–1   SECOND-GRADE LETTER EXCHANGE: JARED AND MRS. WANSART

Dear mrs w
I just read The RunAway
Bunny I really like the
picarse, I have this bouR
m. When my mom read
it tome she sais I am

the Little bunny and
my mom is the mom bunny

I = the main caricters an
mam bunny and Little

bunny the storie takes
pLace in the outdoors

I Like thebunny house

FIGURE 4–1   (CONTINUED)

Dear Jared,
   I read this book to my children at home too. We all really like the story and pictures a lot. I like the way you and your mom pretend to be characters in the story. I like the way the mom always thinks of a way to be with her little bunny if he runs away. Where would you run away to?   Mrs. W.

FIGURE 4–2   THIRD-GRADE LETTER EXCHANGE: MS. BAILEY AND LAUREN

2/17/89   Dear Lauren,

Your table seems to be getting along well together. Are you still happy about it?

What made you decide to leave <u>Harriet The Spy</u>?

That was a clever way for Peggy Parish to start her mystery — by having the children find the first clue in an old hat!! Is there a real Key in the mystery? I'm not sure I understand why or how the children got those presents. Were they a part of buried treasure or a reward?

What are you reading now?

I'm looking forward to learning more about the continents. Today I ordered our encyclopedias, an atlas, a science encyclopedia and some dictionaries for our classroom by using the Readathon money. You all did a really neat job and worked hard Great job!

Well, have a frisky Friday!

Love,
Ms. Bailey

FIGURE 4–2 (CONTINUED)

2/10 ☆ Dear Ms. Bailey,

I gave up on Harrit the spy beacuse It was sort of boring. I'm reading <u>I Want to Live</u> Its starts out liRe this:

Dawn just turned foorteen years old. Her leukemia has been in remission for allmost a year. Her brother Rob is comming for spring. When he comes she has to go to the clinic for tests when she comes home Rob's girlfriend is their. Dawn & mother is having a speial dinner for Rob's girl frenb. Before they start to eat Rob says he's getting with maried with Dorcy. Oops I forgot to ancer all of the questions their is a key for the tresure and the presants are sort of a reward and the tresure

Love,
Louren

FIGURE 4–3   FOURTH-GRADE LETTER EXCHANGE: CHRIS AND MRS. HERDECKER

11/24/87

Dear Mrs. Herdecker,

The Frank family
is in hiding because
they're jewish. The
natzies don't like jewish
people and are sending
them to prison camps.
In the meantime
World War II is going
on. I looked through
my book and I
couldn't find anyplac
where she got in
trouble. I guess she
doesn't get into a
lot of trouble. Right
now in the story
they're talking
about what's
happining in the
world.　　Chris B.

FIGURE 4-3 (CONTINUED)

Dear

Thank you for the explanation, Chris. Very good job!!

You told me in group that you thought your book would <u>influence</u> people who read it. How do you think this will happen? How will the reader be influenced?

How do you feel about that time in history? How do you think Anne Frank must have felt inside as she lived in that attic?

Love,
Mrs. Heidecker

FIGURE 4–3   (CONTINUED)

The Diary of a Young girl
Anne Frank
308
(medium)

12/8/87

Dear Mrs. Herdecker,

I think the reader will be influenced because it will show them to treat people eaqulely.

the classifications I mentioned earlier: easy, medium, and challenging. In this instance, Chris rates Anne Frank's *Diary of a Young Girl* at a medium level of difficulty.

Sometimes children write directly to each other. They don't always solve problems with precision, but they do demonstrate their ability to hypothesize. In Figure 4–4 Chris writes to his friend Sean recommending *Thirty Seconds over Tokyo*. When Sean responds, he questions Chris about the title.

By the time children reach sixth grade and after two years of exchanging letters about their books, the quality and content of the exchanges rise dramatically. The letters are longer and they discuss a broad range of topics. Both the teachers and the children consider how the problems and themes in their reading relate to current issues in their lives. Although the teachers read extensively, they are not able to keep up with the children. This means that they have to ask questions in order to learn more about the child and the book. Teachers work hard to ask children "honest" questions—questions that don't already have answers. If the teacher hasn't read a book, it is a little easier to be honest.

In the sequence depicted in Figure 4–5, Lynn Parsons, a sixth-grade teacher, wonders about John's reading of *The Songs of the Distant Earth*. As she questions him she also mentions the books she is reading. Teachers frequently discuss the books they read with the children; the exchange can be more challenging when it is obvious that both are readers. In her second letter, Ms. Parsons shares her reaction to Roald Dahl's *Matilda*.

In Figure 4–6, Donna Lee, another sixth-grade teacher, discusses her own reading in her letter to Jenn and recommends other books for Jenn to read. From first grade through sixth grade, teachers and children continue to recommend books to each other.

The number of books, the range of reading levels, and the types of books read throughout the school are thought-provoking. When we abolish reading groups and give children as

FIGURE 4–4   FOURTH-GRADE LETTER EXCHANGE: CHRIS AND SEAN

30 seconds over Tokyo
Lawson
179
Medium - Challenge
Dear Mr. SEAN,

I've finished Thirty Seconds over Tokyo and recomend it to someone like you who likes survival. It's about pilots who Bomb Tokyo in 1942. Then while flying to China they crash and have to survive in Villages while Chiniese try to save them from the Japanese. It is pretty exciting when you get into it.

FIGURE 4–4 (CONTINUED)

Dear Mr. CHRIS,
Thanks I might
read it. It sounds
good. If it has
to do with survival
I would probably like
it. Do you know why
it is entitled "Thirty
Seconds Over Tokyo"?
It seemlike a weird
title because bombers
probable didn't spend
30 seconds over Tokyo.

It is called
Thirty Seconds over Tokyo
I think because so
little of the book is
concentrated on the raid.
Most of it is about
their survival in China

FIGURE 4–5   SIXTH-GRADE LETTER EXCHANGE: MS. PARSONS AND JOHN

2/4/89

Dear John,

Hi there! How nice to hear from you and such a nice letter, too! John I'm impressed. The quality of your letters has increased! Are you aware of that? I'm glad!

The Songs of Distant Earth sounds just like your kind of book. I'm glad you enjoyed it! Did you say you borrowed it from your mom? If so, did she read it? Have you discussed it at all with her?

John, did this story take place in the past or the future? It sounds kind of medieval-the way you described it. Yet I also got a futuristic - science fiction feeling from it. What do you think?

I'm still reading Matilda and The Great Alone. I haven't made any progress on Matilda since last week. But I read about 300 pages in The Great Alone. In fact, that's what I did most of Friday! I'm learning a lot about the history of Alaska. In some ways, this book

FIGURE 4–5 (CONTINUED)

reminds me of Sacajawea. Both books deal with varying American Indian tribes.

In <u>The Great Alone</u>, the incredibly vast numbers of seals and sea otter are reduced to dangerously low numbers. In Sacajawea the buffalo herds experienced the same kind of thing. And in <u>both</u> stories, it wasn't the Indians who were responsible. The Indians always were very careful to kill only what they could use. They were very conscious of conservation. They knew they had to be so that there would be buffalo/seals for future generations.

In both stories it was white men who came into the area and massacred thousands and thousands of buffalo and seals. It makes me ashamed that they could be so greedy and thoughtless.

Anyway — I'm really enjoying <u>The Great Alone</u>, and I'm glad I picked it up!

Happy reading!
Love —
Ms. P.

FIGURE 4–5 (CONTINUED)

Dear Mrs. P,   2/8/89

    My mom had previously read <u>The Songs of Distant Earth</u> and she said that she enjoyed it. This story takes place from 3827–3829.

    It was really hard to believe that the spaceship they were travelling in was over 4KM long! There was a real interesting part when the spaceship is leaving Thalassa and there was a blinding flash in the sky. Even when the spaceship is 15 light years away you could still see a faint star that was from the ship's engine which was called a quantam drive. It could power the spaceship at 1/10 the speed of light.

    I am reading <u>The Borrowers</u> by Marry Norton So far it is about three little people that borrow stuff from people to use. What just happened is that Arietty (the youngest of the borrowers) is seen and is talking to the person that caught her.

                 Sincerely,
                 John

FIGURE 4–5 (CONTINUED)

2/9/59

Dear John

Hello! How are you today?

Wow! I can tell by the late date that _The Songs of Distant Earth_ is definately a futuristic story! That spaceship sounds huge. You could almost have a whole town in a spaceship that size.

I've been familiar with the _Borrowers_ for a long time, but I've never read it. Do you think I'd enjoy it? I'm really interested to see how the author would use regular sized items in a miniature home. What are some of the things the borrowers have used from the "big" world?

I've read a little further in _Matilda_. Its about a very smart, very sweet little girl who's parents treat her very badly. When they are particularly

FIGURE 4–5 (CONTINUED)

nasty to her, Matilda does something to get back at them. One
thing she did to her father
was to put Superglue on the inside
of his hat. He can't get it off and
has to shave part of his head to
remove the hat! No one suspect
Matilda!

Happy reading!
Love-
Ms. P.

FIGURE 4–6   SIXTH-GRADE LETTER EXCHANGE: MS. LEE AND JENN

2·6·89

Dear Jenn,

Hi!

Thanks for answering all of my questions. You really wrote a lot last week.

When I read more than one book I often do what you said and focus on the one I'm enjoying most. So, this week I finished <u>Tracker</u> and <u>Writing To Learn</u>. <u>Tracker</u> was beautifully written - capturing the boys views of the forest and hunting as well as his emotions. <u>Writing To Learn</u> exposed me to a number of interesting writers in the fields of ecology, entomology, physics, art, chemistry, music, anthropology, etc... It was fascinating to see that they were all interesting, not just the areas I was already interested in.

What is the <u>Tamcrack Tree</u> about? If it's too boring to read, why don't you try <u>The Upstairs Room</u>. I'm sure you'd like that piece of historical fiction.

Are all of Joan Lowery Nixon's books mysteries? I'd like to try one. I love mysteries

Love,
Ms Lee

FIGURE 4–6   (CONTINUED)

2-12-89

Ms. Lee

As for as I know all of Joan Lowery Nixon's books are mysteries.

The Tamarack Tree is about the civil war. Rosemary is a seventeen year old girl who came to live in Vicksburg, Mississippi with her brother Derek who is 26. She came before the war. RoseMary's parents had died, so RoseMary came from England to live with her brother Derek.

This book is about RoseMary's life which she is writing about. It tells what is happening to her and her brother and what is happening in the war. RoseMary liked living in the south because she made many friends and went to many parties. RoseMary is very mad about slavery; that makes it hard for her to understand her Southern friend's feelings when the war starts.

FIGURE 4–6 (CONTINUED)

It is even harder
for RoseMary when she
finds out her friend, Jeff, who
is from the North, ~~and~~ is
going to join the Union
Army. She is against slavery,
but doesn't want men to
kill each other in a war.
At the part I'm
at now, ~~is~~ RoseMary and
Derek are going to stay in
a cave when the war
starts. Two men dug out
this cave at Dereks
request, so RoseMary and
Derek can stay in the
cave while they're at
war. Derek said " It's better
to stay in a cave then
stay in your house and
have the roof cave in. "
Now they are
going to stay in the cave
so they can get use to
it before the war.

Jenn

FIGURE 4–6   (CONTINUED)

2-13-89

Dear Jenn,

Hi! What an interesting letter!

I can't imagine why this book is so boring - your description of the plot makes it sound anything but dull. It would be very interesting to have an outsider observing the conflict. By the way, is Derek going to be expected to fight for the south?

Is Jeff her boyfriend, or a friend? Is she still in contact with him?

How large is the cave? How comfortable is it?

In a successful piece of historical fiction the author creates realistic characters and also teaches about that time in history. Are you learning a lot about this time in history? What do you find interesting about this time period?

FIGURE 4–6   (CONTINUED)

I've been reading The Education of Little Tree. Ms. Stockley loaned it to me. It's an autobiography about a young Cherokee boy being raised by his grandparents. They try to teach him the beliefs and values of Cherokee people. So far it's pretty interesting and beautifully written.

Love,
Ms. Lee

much as forty-five to fifty-five minutes of straight reading time, it is not unusual for them to read from thirty to ninety books in a year's time. More important than the number, however, is the children's growing ability to be critical about their reading and to relate books to their everyday lives. Because they have a choice about the books they read, the level of difficulty in the books they choose continues to climb, and the range of their reading exceeds what might be required in any school curriculum guide. The basis of this entire venture, however, is the literate life of the teacher, who is constantly reading and sharing books with the children.

ACTION: RETHINK SKILLS.

Children pick up many of the skills of literacy through their writing. When children "invent" their spellings, they demonstrate one of the best examples of applied learning for sound/symbol relationships. When the classroom is decentralized and highly structured, children can help each other, thus providing maximum opportunity for both teaching and learning about word and meaning problems.

Teachers can also conduct mini-lessons on important learning tools that will help children when they read. A mini-lesson is a five- to ten-minute demonstration of a helpful tool to a small group or to the entire class. The following are examples of reading mini-lessons:

- Prediction: reading the opening of a book or a story and predicting possible outcomes based on early evidence.
- "When I don't understand the word": demonstrating strategies for uncovering the meaning of unknown words.
- How authors handle characters, dialogue, plot, leads or openings, setting, endings: each of these is a separate mini-lesson, and there is obvious overlap with writing.
- Working with the paragraph: showing how to make paragraphs from straight copy of a child's piece.

- Choosing books: how to know if a book is easy, in the middle, or difficult.
- Using the dictionary, encyclopedia, library.

ACTION: LET CHILDREN SHARE IN YOUR READING.

Children need to know how your reading affects you. At book sharing time, periodically tell the children about the books you are reading so they can see how books enter into the life of an adult. This type of sharing is not intended to bring up deep, personal issues or problems in your life, but rather to show how books can enrich everyday enjoyments, discuss issues, or give needed information.

So much of learning is through apprenticeship. When children see how teachers read, how reading strikes them, how they discover new books and give reading an important place in their lives, they answer the greatest question—"Why would anyone want to read?"—every day.

The evidence is strong that the reading habits of parents have a great influence on their children's reading, both their desire and their growth as effective readers. If it is parents' literate engagement with the world through speaking, reading, writing, and listening that largely determines a child's literate future, is the teacher's any less important? For many children, the teacher is the one adult they encounter in their lives who has a questioning, literate engagement with the world.

FINAL REFLECTION   Reading is for everyone. It is not a subject. It is not something people do in circles and groups determined by ability or specific skill weaknesses. It is not something that should require children to complete twenty skill sheets in a day. One child expressed his impatience quite directly: "I can't wait to finish reading so I can read!"

Reading is visiting the planets, countries, and dramas behind the words children learn quickly because they need them.

Through extended, self-directed practice, children read because their friends and teachers do. They read in order to share the new friends they meet in books with their classmates. They read to demonstrate what they know about sharks, lasers, Honduras, dogs, cats, and cheetahs. Because they have time to read in school, they tunnel into books; then they read them at home and talk about them with their friends. They read even when they are not reading as their minds scroll through the events and images of heroic deeds and speculate on the outcome of mysteries, stories, or the biographies of the people they wish to become.

We have been seduced into believing that reading is meant to be a complicated process requiring highly systematic, step-by-step procedures and stimulus/response-type activities that suggest a false mastery of component parts. Make no mistake, for some children reading can be a perplexing, complicated, trying act. Especially for these children, however, learning, sharing, and enjoying the writing of other authors is all-important.

Teachers read for themselves and to keep up with children. They have discovered that when they let the children do what they themselves already practice, the quality of their thinking and their literate engagement with the world change dramatically. For Paula Walsh, children's personal victories and change as learners have been incentive enough:

PAULA: One child came into my class with his head down. He was in next to the lowest group. And now he reads every minute that he can. When reading time starts, he's ready. He may read at his desk or in the quiet corner. He uses every single minute. I ask him, "Keith, tell me about the book you are reading." And he makes eye contact with me and he has a lot to say. He used to give just yes or no answers. Now, it is like touching a button when I say, "Tell me about your reading."

Most of us went into teaching because we wished to share in children's learning, to contribute somehow to making it happen. My image of the teacher (as an English major) was that of an enthusiastic, dynamic individual who paced the room lecturing and telling children of the wonders of literature and watched them race to the library when the bell rang. I never knew that teaching was simply a matter of letting children read, inquiring into their thinking, following their interests, allowing them to share with their classmates, and challenging and encouraging their dreams.

listen to teach

Listening is at the heart of learning for both children and teacher. Unless we listen we have no window on the world. We can see, touch, and feel, but the world of words is lost to us. But if we are to live the life of words in our teaching and in our writing, we need to hear the words of children and adults, both when they speak and when they write.

I listen with "two ears": to the words of children speaking and, simultaneously, to my own inner voice as it translates children's utterances into insights and into questions, as it shuttles back and forth over my own experience as a writer, teacher, and liver of many lives. As children speak, they trigger my awareness of the many selves within me: reader, parent, teacher—and child again.

Some days I fight to maintain my objectivity. When Angela tearfully describes her piece about her cat, which was given away by her mother, I worry about what I will say to her, so much so that I cease to hear her speaking. Or I know so well what I think I should say that I don't hear her last words of cheerful resolution on the matter.

On another day, Joshua speaks of his willingness to share his piece with the group and gives several reasons why it is ready. I am prepared for this moment, and I savor every word. I listen well because I have thirsted so long for this willingness to share, and I forget myself. I hear his words as we lock eyes; later, I remember every detail of his face and every word he spoke.

Angela and Joshua need to discover their own voices, and the written voice is first heard in speech. Voices need audiences. The teacher works hard to show children how to be an audience by being a good listener herself. They will become good listeners if she takes time to show them how, if she hears their words and then uses the same words to ask questions that will help them say other words they didn't know they could say.

In this way, the children become a community as they learn

to write and speak about what they know. They listen to each other because they have learned to listen to themselves, and they have learned to listen to themselves by listening to the other children in their classroom. Because their classmates have listened to their writing, told them what they heard, and asked questions, the authors discover that they know much more than they thought they did when they wrote.

We live in a world that has not learned to listen. Each year, some new product adds to the cacophony of our lives: audio- and videotapes, portable radios, records, and compact discs produce an almost constant hum. Yet communication at best is one-way: we speak *at* each other. In addition, a self-centered authoritativeness seems to be the order of the day, a difficult model for learning to listen. For these reasons too many of us who teach have learned to speak at others and to listen more passively to those forms of media that do not demand a response.

Teachers also need a *professional* world that listens to them. When the popular press second-guesses their work, when mandates are issued from school boards and memos that reflect little consultation with staff come from the desks of school administrators, and when school policies make teachers focus on objectives in the future, on end-of-year scores, on getting ready for the next teacher, teachers cannot pay attention to their daily responses to the individual children in their classrooms.

Real listening requires that teachers focus with care and full attention on the moment the child speaks. They can do so only if they are experienced in listening to their own writing and reading, to the writing of children who work to construct whole pieces out of a few words, or to children's chance remarks. Every focused moment of listening adds to the particular reading and writing histories of both child and teacher. From these shared histories they begin to construct plans for the future.

Preparation and discipline are behind the "listening moment" between child and teacher. The teacher has experienced the writing/reading process and understands the meaning of what she hears; she has designed the classroom so that children can assume responsibility for listening to each other, working independently, and not interrupting her when she is listening.

This chapter will focus on eight Actions:

- Learn to listen to yourself.
- Write about a literate occasion and watch/listen for your own voice.
- Discover your voice as you read.
- Explore other opportunities to practice watching and listening for your own voice.
- Look for children's voices throughout the day.
- Practice when it is appropriate *not* to listen.
- Review your day for difficult listening occasions.
- Plan to evolve as a listener.
- Help children learn how to listen.

ACTION: LEARN TO LISTEN TO YOURSELF.

Despite the fact that I'm well into my fifties, I recently decided that after twenty-one years of cross-country running, I needed to diversify my exercise program. I decided to enter the world of cycling. Although I hadn't owned a bicycle since high school and, to the best of my recollection, had only sat on one three times since my graduation from bicycles to automobiles, I went out to buy a bicycle.

I entered the bicycle shop a bit breathless and voiceless, not because I was afraid of cycling, but because I was worried about looking like a middle-aged fool in shorts when I began to ask questions about bicycles. The proprietor sensed my state and gave me what he must have thought were elementary explanations of the various types of bicycles and the advantages and disadvantages of each. He spoke about alloyed and steel-frame components, ten and twelve speeds, handlebar placement, braking systems, weight, and safety features.

I barely processed what he was saying. He knew so much; I knew so little. He wasn't overbearing; in fact, he was a good teacher. But his advice made me see even more clearly that I didn't know anything about bicycles. I had no opinions and only a few meager facts. Yet I wanted to get on the road.

I needed to talk about bicycles. Three times I interrupted the proprietor to tell him what I had just learned, knowing I'd make some mistakes in trying to make his information mine—and I made them. I couldn't understand the meaning of a one-pound weight difference between bicycles or the advantage of alloys over nonalloys. The gears were a complete wipeout: I didn't know a high gear from a low one or a large sprocket from a small one. Still, I needed to make a decision. I needed to exercise my voice, place my meager knowledge on the line, purchase a bicycle, and get on the road.

I needed to read about bicycles, cycle extensively, talk about bicycles, and write about bicycles, as I am doing now. This is how I discover the edges of my thinking; I push my thinking —on gear ratios, for example—to the point of fuzziness, and then I read and ask others for more information about, say, the best ways to shift from low to high using the two front sprockets. As the details fall into place, as I discover the edges of my thought, I begin to have opinions and feelings—about whether to have brakes in two locations or to cycle leaning into the handlebars or sitting vertically in the saddle.

The next time I visited the bicycle shop after cycling daily for two weeks, reading a book on cycling, and talking with other cyclists, I talked and listened differently. My voice as a cyclist began to emerge; best of all, I began to listen with "two ears": "this is what he is saying, this is what I think." I became aware of the process of engagement, of the distinctions between voices, and of new questions to ask.

Learning to listen to myself required action: I asked ill-formed questions, practiced, formulated more questions, read, and practiced some more. I became more aware of what worked and didn't work for me. I also had to figure out where cycling fit into my overall life scheme. Every day I had to face the most important question: "Why cycle at all?"

Developing a listening voice, that sense of self that says "that's where they are; here's where I am," starts as soon as I begin to read something new or listen to another person speak about her writing. If this new voice is tentative in its judgments, it is audacious in its questions, constantly seeking to formulate further questions that will embrace a subject, however elusive it seems. The new voice demands facts. For the learner, shifts in voice are evidence of growth. They say, "Aha, I'm on the right track to . . . a whole new idea, a whole new way of looking at things."

I develop my own voice through details and facts, solid information that confirms my perceptions and judgments. Writing about the literate occasions I encounter (see Chapter 3) is a great help in establishing voice—that sense of the self in relation to the facts and details at hand. I record *what* I see and hear as well as my reaction. For at least ten to fifteen minutes a day, I pull away from my daily routines to listen and reflect. My writing becomes my laboratory for thinking.

I also clip articles that interest me out of newspapers and magazines and underline the lines I like and dislike. I superimpose my voice on the writer's voice with a word, or a note to myself or to a friend: "You'll like this," or "Doesn't this make your blood boil?"

ACTION: WRITE ABOUT A LITERATE OCCASION AND WATCH/LISTEN FOR YOUR OWN VOICE.

The notion of listening needs to be more carefully described. I'll use a recent personal example to show what I mean. Five days ago I went through the unusual experience of passing a kidney stone. A number of firsts went with the event. It was my first time in the hospital and my first encounter with real pain. At several points during peaks of pain, the notion "Am I ever going to write about this?" flickered through my mind. The experience was too intense to be understood at the time.

When I finally wrote about it, I listened to my inner voice as it probed and questioned. But it was more than listening. I watched. I went back to that moment as if I had "instant replay" capabilities and watched myself on the X-ray table. I watched the nurses, doctors, and technicians. I'll write in double columns to show what I mean. In the left column are the words I wrote about the occasion itself, and in the right column those I wrote about the process of seeing and listening.

I lay on the gurney in the hospital emergency room. I didn't have an emergency but that's where you end up if you don't have a personal doctor to see you. On the other side of the canvas curtain surrounding my cubicle I heard the voice of a man saying, "Oh, oh, oh what am I going to do?" He'd be quiet for a while and then start to moan again. I thought, "He must be that young bearded man who came into the Emergency room with one leg dragging and supported by two people."

As I wrote about that very brief moment I saw myself on the gurney, heard the voice, then realized that I didn't actually see the man. You, the reader, also popped in. You said, "How come you were in the emergency room?" You'd want to know, and I had to answer that question before you would read on. Something was separating me from that man. Yes, the canvas curtain. It may not have been canvas but it appeared to be heavy. When I couldn't see him, I remember staring at that curtain with the slight chance that it might be open and I'd catch a glimpse of that young man in pain. I was anxious to know if he was

> *the same man I'd observed earlier.*
>
> *Notice that this is a combination of unfolding pictures and voice. My voice runs along the picture, probing with questions, "What do I see? Why did I keep looking at the canvas? Who is that man?" The listening to myself comes in when I try to answer my own questions, but I don't write down the questions. Rather, what the reader gets are the answers to my questions.*

For this Action, write for ten minutes about an occasion you know you will share with someone. When you finish, write a brief, five-minute reflection about what you saw and how you reported it. Be aware of how you listened to yourself as you put words down on the page.

ACTION: DISCOVER YOUR VOICE AS YOU READ.

When I read, I watch and listen just as I do when I write. I'll take a passage in a book I'm reading right now to show what I mean. The book is *The Power of Myth*, an edited series of interviews between Bill Moyers and the philosopher Joseph Campbell that were aired on public television. What's in the right-hand column is the result of my listening to the text and to myself in response to the text. Because I am writing down my response, it is probably a more limited version of what went on in my mind when I read. Still, I will try to record, as well as I can recall, the thoughts, images, and voices I encountered as I read. I will share what happened when I listened to myself.

MOYERS: *How did you get them [students] interested in myths?*

CAMPBELL: *Young people just grab this stuff. Mythology teaches you what's behind literature and the arts, it teaches you about your own life. It's a great, exciting, life-nourishing subject. Mythology has a great deal to do with the stages of life, the initiation ceremonies as you move from childhood to adult responsibilities, from the unmarried state into the married state. All of those rituals are mythological rites. They have to do with your recognition of the new role that you're in, the process of throwing off the old one and coming out in the new, and entering into a responsible profession.*

When a judge walks into the room, and everybody stands up, you're not standing up to that guy, you're standing up to the

What's Campbell up to here? What's he bringing together? Students and why they like mythology, I guess. Yes, they ask questions of their own if Campbell asks big questions. And Campbell does. He shows how the subject is bigger than he is, and the students know that. There is plenty of room to explore. The students crave edges to life and sense that they are on a defined trip, the stages of life. Trouble is there is none of that in our culture as there used to be. There are few markers separating students from children or people in their eighties. There is no becoming. I see a classroom full of students, their faces open and asking "how come?" I see a student alone in a dorm, head down, very discouraged. No answers to life. I feel for that student.

The judge, now I see Judge Wapner because yesterday I saw Rain Man. *But there is the judge, and Campbell has given me an image. And I remember.*

robe that he's wearing and the role that he's going to play. What makes him worthy of that role is his integrity, as a representative of the principles of that role, and not some group of prejudices of his own. So what you're standing up to is a mythological character. I imagine some kings and queens are the most stupid, absurd, banal people you could run into, probably interested only in horses and women, you know. But you're not responding to them as personalities, you're responding to them in their mythological roles. When someone becomes a judge, or President of the United States, the man is no longer that man, he's the representative of an eternal office; he has to sacrifice his personal desires and even life possibilities to the role that he now signifies.

a judge who wasn't any of this unbiased stuff, a woman judge in Dade County, Florida, on ''60 Minutes'' who gave maximum sentences to the guilty. A tough bird and I thought her very unfair because of the prejudice she brought to the bench and freely admitted. And then at the end of the paragraph I saw myself put in a kind of mythological role when I speak to large audiences. People talk to me not as the Don Graves I know but as the person in the role of the man who just spoke on the stage, and I realize that is all they can do. The role puts me in a category that requires a kind of behavior I don't necessarily want. A mythology is born here and I am caught up in it.

I tried to follow Campbell's exposition and produce my own examples. I see students in classrooms, alone in the dorm, or at graduation. When I read, I seem to need to conjure up images, even in the midst of exposition. Perhaps that's why I read so slowly. I've also produced a parallel text about what happens when there are no obvious cultural stages, a kind of translation of Campbell's ideas for myself.

I read to listen to myself, to see what I see. Campbell's words made it possible for me to make an even greater personal connection in the second paragraph. In one sense, each of us participates in a mythology in our roles as parents, grandparents, teachers, and professors. While I wrote, I watched myself listening to Campbell, but my listening was shaped by my audience. I knew I'd be writing about my reading and probably listened better than if I had sat in my easy chair alone by the fire.

Every one of you who reads the passage by Campbell produced different images as well as different questions. Perhaps some of you imagined no images at all and were only aware of your reading voice. Others may have complained about Campbell's statements, saying that they were too abstract or dealt with questions that were irrelevant to your interests. My wife, Betty, read the same selection and came up with this rendition of what went through her mind.

I'm middle class and I'm not interested in myth. Can he make this interesting for me? We'll see. I must be missing something if he thinks it is so important and vital for young people. He talks about it coming through the stages of life. Ceremonies of life, baptism, marriage, old age. Is he going to do this? Oh, his logic is the same logic as mine. We're on the same wavelength.

Myths will tell me how to grow up, how to go from one stage to the other in life. The mythology I know is biblical—Joseph, the biblical scene with palm trees and Joseph in his many-colored coat, and camels walking over sand dunes. I see them. Those mythological stories that I take for granted. There's a deeper meaning in those than just the story. I have to think about that sometime.

Kings and queens. Queen Elizabeth and the difference between the person in crown and royal regalia, the diamond star of authority on that ribbon across her bosom, contrasted with her watching the races in Scotland and a peasant kerchief on her head and the tension between the press and the picture the family royalty wants to present. And I'm thinking of Reagan and his privacy when he has bowel surgery and his Hollywood actor status and how he presents the myth side because he knows how to present an imagined leader role which he doesn't fulfill in reality.

Here is another account of the very same passage with images and comments very different from my own. And this is as it should be. Both of us struggled with the meaning of myth, and Moyer and Campbell allowed us to travel a different, yet parallel journey. I couldn't resist asking Betty about the part on judges and black robes. That section triggered off a host of images for me; why not for her? She said, "Oh, those black robes were dull and uninteresting. Nothing happened for me in that paragraph until I came to kings and queens. The queen in regalia, the myth surrounding the costume really set me off. And then Reagan came in very naturally."

In Betty's case, and to some degree in mine, there was an early struggle for text relevancy with learner questions: Will he deliver? Can I deliver? When she produces a trial construct on the stages of life and myth, Campbell's text falls right into it. Betty has always been a better reader than I am. She has a voice that probes and confirms. No images or pictures came to her until her Joseph scene, but then they were followed by Queen Elizabeth and then Ronald Reagan. Her inner reflections reveal parts of a personal narrative that work with these three scenes.

ACTION: EXPLORE OTHER OPPORTUNITIES TO PRACTICE WATCHING AND
LISTENING FOR YOUR OWN VOICE.

When you listen to your own voice, recognize that you are a seer. You are someone who notices details about your world and the events that unfold in it. What you observe triggers thoughts and feelings. As you comment on what you see, you are aware that your comments, both oral and written, begin to sound like you.

The following Actions will help you practice listening to yourself:

• Observe an event with someone. Without speaking to each other write a short, five-minute account of what you have seen. Then write for two minutes, commenting on the meaning of what you have seen.
• Attend a faculty meeting and make a list of the positions on one issue and the details used to support them. Be sure to provide a list of your own positions.

ACTION: LOOK FOR CHILDREN'S VOICES THROUGHOUT THE DAY.

I listen for facts and I listen for feelings. Sometimes I hear strong voices on the playground and weak voices in the classroom, and I want to know why. Craig is enraged at the injustice of a bad call in a playground game. He has feelings; I want Craig to tell me the details of what happened, the facts that stand behind his feelings. Emily has just shared some facts from her book about brown bears; I want to know what she thinks of those facts. Were they useful? Did they surprise her? Did they make her think of other questions? Both Craig and Emily know that, above all, I want details, their own reactions to what they think. I must put my voice to one side, at the same time recognizing that it is present in both my listening and my questioning.

Good teachers do have voices and opinions, but the strength of each is enhanced twofold when children know that the teacher is interested in what they have to say. Strong voices listening to emerging voices show the highest form of respect. And teachers who write, who have a writer's sense of themselves—of what they think and how they think it—can have a still more powerful effect on children who write when they want to learn more.

I look for moments in the school day when children can be children. In class, they are used to school-type routines and often don't feel as free to express themselves. So I try to be part of their informal day. I go out on the playground with the children at recess. I watch for physical abilities, social groupings, and negotiations over play; I also watch for children who function well in the formal structure of the classroom but pull away from the unpredictable play that occurs at recess. Above all, I listen for children's voices when they speak their minds about incidents outdoors that they might not speak about indoors. I look for the specifics in these incidents that have shaped their feelings, hoping where appropriate to help children understand their experiences.

I do the same at lunchtime, while children wait in lines for music programs or physical education, during rehearsals—during all the informal activities that make up a school day. Then I write notes to the children to show that I have listened. I carry a small pad of the yellow, stick-on notes that are sold in most stationery stores, and I write down one- or two-sentence messages: "I noticed that you scored a goal today in soccer." "You helped Bill and took his side." "You finished a book today and shared it with Angela." I want children to know that I see and hear the *details*, the essentials of living that are important to their development as persons.

ACTION: PRACTICE WHEN IT IS APPROPRIATE *NOT* TO LISTEN.

There are limits to listening, and children have to learn them. Children and teachers have to learn them together. Children who are not used to having adult listeners in their lives can be overly reliant on them. Sometimes a ten-page piece must be listened to word by word, or a ten-minute story of what happened on the playground must be heard in its entirety. Most of the time, however, it is not a good use of the child's or the teacher's time. I don't want children to need me so much that I have to listen to an entire piece. Often I counter with a question: "Have you shared this with a friend?" "What do you want me to listen to?" "What part is the most important?" "Why is this an important time to listen?" The child may come up with an appropriate answer, and then I do listen. At other times I simply may not have time: "We'll have to talk about that later."

Listening isn't listening unless there are boundaries to it. Inappropriate or ill-timed listening has to be defined. I want children to discuss differences of opinion until matters are settled, but not all things are negotiable at all times: "Today, Mark, you are to go outside to recess. We can't negotiate."

When I am listening intently to one child, I am not to be interrupted by another child; except for an extreme emergency, this is not negotiable. Most of the time I will ignore a child's interference and discuss the matter with that child later. If I negotiate with one child while trying to listen to the child in front of me, I have not drawn a line.

Children need to be able to draw the line on listening as well. Throughout the year I deliberately set the room up so that children can learn to listen to and offer help to each other. I listen to them to help them develop their own voices and, in turn, I expect them to do the same for each other. But there are limits.

Some children may be just beginning a piece. They may have difficulty getting the piece to move. Or they may have had a series of conferences with other children and see their time running out on a deadline. A few children have an unusual listening burden simply because they are good listeners, but there are days when these good listeners need to be on their own without any interference. For occasions like these, I provide a place in the room for children who need a "time-out" location, a place of noninterference from others, where no one can bother them, including the teacher.

Most of the time, children decide when to go to the "silent" or "time-out" area. They know when they need it. The basic rules are that those in the silent area are not to speak to anyone else there, and no one in the room can speak to them. There are times, however, when I'll ask a child if the "silent" area might be helpful. I find that children who are moving in a piece use it more because they're at a point where interference isn't desirable. Younger children who are stuck on a piece and can't get started usually need to talk; for them the silent area doesn't work. There are children, however, who find that a quiet area suits their learning style and the way they solve problems.

The quiet area is something I frequently talk over with the class. "How did the quiet area help you? When do you find it helpful?" I want a variety of responses, since the range of uses for the quiet area enhances its strength. I'll also ask, "How can we improve its use? Is it located in the best spot?"

I also find that the "no listening" area is useful for diagnostic purposes. I need to know about children's varying habits, who needs no listening at a particular time, and so on. On occasion I may even enter the quiet area myself to write or think.

ACTION: REVIEW YOUR DAY FOR DIFFICULT LISTENING OCCASIONS.
Listening is most difficult when I feel the pressure of time or the curriculum. It is also difficult when I am oriented more to the future than to the present, when I listen to a child while thinking automatically of the next child, of how many children I can see in a morning (I'm already behind . . .). The curriculum problem comes up when I feel the pressure of finding ways for the children to be "touched" by the curriculum. It's like picking up a book I'm assigned to read and becoming so preoccupied

with finishing it that I find myself on page 3 without having really read anything yet. My eyes see words but I don't read them. I see children but I don't listen to them. When I sense that my concern about the future has taken over the very important present, I have to rethink the importance of listening itself. Listening helps us spot the child's voice and supply the spark that will help the child to write, to know her own voice. When I listen, I am looking for what a child has to offer, what a child knows, in order to help that child share it, either orally or in writing. I approach the child with the expectation that she knows something, that a discovery for each of us—child and teacher—is just around the corner.

Listening is difficult when I feel overly responsible for a child's learning. I say to myself, "He isn't doing well; what's wrong with me? I don't seem to be a very good teacher for him." Without listening I become directive. I take over a child's learning. "Here, let's get away from all those topics about sports. Write about your dog. And I don't care for all those misspellings. Go use the dictionary." There are those moments when teachers need to be directive. But I am referring to the urge to correct instead of teach, to seemingly speed up the process of learning.

Listening is difficult when children write about what *I* know. I have the urge to make the child live up to the subject as I know it, not as she needs to learn it. If I know about gardening, I try to show the child how much I know, so that she might respect my "gardening voice" rather than her own. For some strange reason, I am so insecure as a learner that I feel the need to use my learning to impress a child rather than to ask good questions that will reveal to the child what she already knows. When I find myself taking over a child's piece, and when my knowledge base is strong, then it points to my need to work on developing my own voice. This is a common example of the lack of "dual track" listening. If you recognize yourself here, work hard to understand your own voice and reconsider the first three Actions in this chapter.

ACTION: PLAN TO EVOLVE AS A LISTENER.

Learning to listen well is a lifelong task. But you can begin today to reap some of the benefits along the way. You can begin to keep a journal in which you write down brief observations about anything that strikes you and record your reactions to those events. Ten to fifteen minutes a day will be enough to start. The beginning may be no more than recall:

John is off track today. He's angry about something. He charged around the playground and kept on poking whoever was in front of him in line. Come to think of it, he was angry when he came in the door. Must have been something before he came to school. I'll ask him what it was.

Read short piece about reading in Language Arts. *The writer never seems to have gotten started. It may be me but the writer assumed too much.*

You can begin to listen to the children by simply hearing their statements, repeating the essence of what they have said or written back to them, and asking, "Is that what you said? Is that what you wrote?" If you've missed something, the children will let you know. Listen to your colleagues in the teachers' room or in the corridor. Strive for accuracy in listening: "Do I have the essence of what you said?" Keep your value judgments to yourself, but be aware of what they are. Note that you are not asking direct questions yet.

Do the same with the children when they write. The first two weeks you will probably do no more than walk around the room responding to their pieces. "Oh, I see you are writing about sharks. . . . Here's one on Gobots. . . . Wendy, you have quite a bit of information here about muskrats, how they build their homes, what they eat, how they raise their young." Focus on details wherever you find them.

As soon as you feel comfortable responding to children's work, begin to ask questions to help them teach you about what they know. Look at a child's piece to see what information it reveals and whether that information may have still more behind it. Your early questions seek to help the child to control the information and to begin to get words on the paper. Later, you may ask more penetrating questions, questions more fundamental to handling the demands of the information.

On the first day, pick five to seven children, those whom you find it easiest to listen to; these children probably aren't stuck in their writing and have more details down on paper. Before you listen or respond, make it clear that you are not to be interrupted.

ACTION: HELP CHILDREN LEARN HOW TO LISTEN.

You learn to listen to yourself and to children because you want them to learn to do the same. Try to demonstrate good listening, although you know many of the children come from different listening traditions, because your own demonstrations are a dominant force in how children view learning. To help children learn to listen, try some of the following: (1) Practice listening to the oral and written utterances of children. (2) Confirm the children's individual voices. (3) Encourage a growing sense of community. Try these simultaneously. None is more important than another.

Practice with listening comes through responding to and questioning children's writing. At the end of the writing period, two to three children can share their pieces with the entire class. When a piece is shared, the author calls on other children who report on what struck them in the piece: in some instances they tell what they remember, in others they tell what impressed them and what they liked. The point of this sharing session is to help the author discover what the audience took away from the reading. The author wants to know that he has been heard. At the same time, the audience seeks to sit where the author sat when the piece was written. When the group finishes responding to the piece, children ask clarifying questions to satisfy their own curiosity and to help the author. "How did you happen to write this piece?" "What will you do with it?" "Are you going to publish this?" "How come he wasn't sad when his dog died?" "What was the hardest part to write?" They usually want to know about both the process and the content.

Sharing helps writers to clarify content while hearing their own voice speak about the subject and hearing it come back to them through the class's response and questioning. When the other children ask questions and thus confirm a piece, writers learn what voice is. The teacher participates in this process along with the children when he raises his hand to ask questions and to learn from a child sharing writing on a particular day. More and more, children should be able to say, "This is what *I* think; this is what *they* think." Sharing is the process of confirming individual voices. Until I feel that my voice has been heard, it is hard to hear the voices of others. And when children discover that the details in their writing can affect others, they find it easier to listen to the writing of others.

As a teacher, I work overtime to establish the specifics of what individual children know. I carry the names of all the children in my head, hoping to post on my mental list more details about children's experiences, strong attributes, and personal concerns. The details are crucial; these are precisely what I want to confirm for children when they read their writing aloud—and thus confirm their ability. The more details I use, the more I contribute to children's sense of themselves as persons. Children who listen to other children are highly articulate about what those children know and how they know it. Not only do they pick up new strategies and acquire a broad base of knowledge, but they begin to participate in a real learning community. Communities are born through an exchange of information that is meant to help both individual members and the community as a whole. The quality of the listening that goes on in the group determines the quality of the community. The more children discover their own unique voices, the more the group can discover its own identity.

FINAL REFLECTION Teachers who learn to listen to themselves are confident about their own voice and better equipped to hear the voices of others and to help children do the same. The individual human voice reveals itself in what it says—in speech and writing. Through voice, we show what we know, what we think, and how we think it.

Good listening requires that we separate ourselves from the person speaking. We need to recognize that, although we have real opinions of our own, we need to set them aside in order to hear what the speaker is saying. Most of us don't recognize where the speaker's ideas end and ours begin. It takes work to notice the distinction.

Teachers prepare to be good listeners by becoming conscious of their own voices. They read, write, keep journals, and record their own reactions to what they think and feel. This also prepares them to understand where children are in their writing; they have shared writing in class groups and know what it is like to be on the other side. They can say, "This is what I think; this is what the group thinks."

Teachers who listen to themselves begin to learn how to focus on the listening moment. They learn how to recognize in the details of a child's simple utterances possibilities for helping that child discover her own voice. They can ask questions of children who express general feelings in their writing to show them how to include the details that back up those feelings. They can look for precise verbs and nouns in children's writing and urge them to include more, while respecting the right of the writer to refuse until he is ready.

There are times when teachers shouldn't listen and times when listening is hard. Teachers can't often listen to readings of very long pieces. They can't listen to many children when they are focusing on what one child is saying. Classrooms need a quiet place where children can work without needing to listen to others. For both teachers and children, there must be established limits to listening if listening is to have any importance at all.

As teachers, we help children develop listening skills so that they can learn to hear their own inner voice and the voices of other writers and speakers. They get formal help when they learn to respond to what other children say, read, and write and when they ask questions. But first they work hard to sit where the author sat to see the world from that point of view. Teachers work hard to help children recognize and develop the details of what they know. When children know they know something—know what they think and why they think that way—they are usually able to help other children. A listening and learning community emerges in those classrooms where children possess a wide variety of strategies for learning and an abundance of knowledge that they have acquired from each other.

experiment with learning

Learning is a way of life for teachers and even more so for the literate person who wishes to teach reading and writing. "Of course I'm a learner," you may say, and you're right. Today people can hardly get out of bed without confronting something new: how to use an 800 telephone number, how the school bus schedule works, how to follow the directions for assembling a new toy, how to figure out the supermarket's latest logic for arranging the aisles, how to set the timer on a video recorder, or how to punch in the code to use the bank cash machine.

Teachers who are learners like to watch themselves learn. These professionals are as much students of learning itself as they are of reading, listening, and writing. When I listen to the words on the page as I write about a literate occasion, I not only learn from the information I jot down, I also watch myself learning to learn.

The literate life, however, includes far more than reading and writing. Literate people have a passion for asking questions, both big and small, a hunger for learning new things and for making connections. In short, they have a particular stance toward the universe: one of constant engagement and learning.

The literate life makes me ask questions: what place does the family have in our society? What is my responsibility toward world hunger? What does it mean to be responsible to the land on which I live? How can I be a good neighbor, father, husband, grandfather, son? What's right? What's wrong? I have much to learn in pursuing answers to these questions.

Then there is that part of the literate life that propels me to learn specific crafts and tasks. Not all learning results from solving daily problems. I want my learning repertoire to include deliberate decisions to learn something new. Perhaps I've wanted to learn to play the piano, find out about wine or French cooking, move into photography or sketching, or try water skiing or aerobics. I want to be more conscious of learning, to mess around in something new, to be a little closer to the learning edge. This chapter will move you into Actions that

105

make you conscious of your learning history and carry you into new learning experiences.

ACTION: REVIEW YOUR LEARNING HISTORY.

Six years ago, I started working on a book about teaching and learning that is still going strong. While writing about my Great Uncle Nelson in *Writing: Teachers & Children at Work,* I remembered the way he taught me how to launch and scull a boat, tie a bowline, and tell if a rope had been snapped or cut. How he taught and how I learned were teaching/learning events. In the first Action I invite you to find out some of your own learning history before you take on the next Action, learning something new.

To understand my learning history, I started with a three-column format (see Figure 6–1). In the first column I listed some simple things I'd learned, such as the earliest I remember, learning to tie my shoe. In the second column I put the name of the person who taught me that process or skill. In the third column ("Notes") I put down a few words that were associated with the learning event to help me recall the teaching/learning story. You can design a similar chart for yourself.

What my chart helped me see was that the simpler the learning event, the more I found out about good teaching and learning. But although it was a help to me, I didn't actually understand the teaching and the learning until I had written out what had gone on. Here are two examples (items 1 and 8 from Figure 6–1) to show what I mean. They are both abbreviated accounts of my written text.

NO. 1

When I was about six years old, in first grade anyway, my mother announced, "Donald, it is time you learned to tie your shoes by yourself." She led me into the living room and told me to stand in front of the arm of the couch. The couch had an arm with a rest attaching it to the main couch about ten inches back so that it stood out like an arm. She placed me directly in front of the arm, at

FIGURE 6–1   LEARNING HISTORY

Learning	Person	Notes
1. Tie shoe	Mother	Couch; bathrobe tie; Weehawken, N. J.
2. Direction sense	Dad	Walking streets in Weehawken.
3. Make bed	Mother	Hospital corners; E. Greenwich, R. I.
4. Scull a boat	Uncle Nelson	Wilbur's Point; how to keep oar in slot.
5. Drive a car	Grandpa Hiller	Fairhaven; big Buick.
6. That I was American	Leo Hecke	A Nazi, who helped me realize I was American, and not something else; Joe Louis fight.
7. Concept of money	Mother	First bank; budget envelopes; E. Greenwich, R. I.
8. Hit golf ball	Pro	New York; first lesson, hit bucket of balls.

my age slightly below eye level. She took the broad sash from her robe and said, "Watch what I do. I put this around the arm, then I take the ends, put one end over and under the other. Now you try it." She took my hands, placed them just in back of the ends and put one over, the other under. The tie for her robe was much thicker than my flimsy shoestrings, and I could see the whole operation at near eye level. "Now you do it." And I did. From here she went on to the loops. Within a few days I was able to gauge down to the little strings and tie my shoes by myself.

NO. 8

I remember learning to hit a golf ball. A few weeks into trying to play golf, I set aside some money to pay for instructions from a pro. I expected to see a lean, blond-haired Jack Nicklaus. Instead, a man with a paunch and a cigar took me out to the fairway. I was an English major, liked words, and expected a lecture on how to hit a golf ball. Instead, he said, "Here's a bucket of balls. Hit 'em." I teed up, swung at some balls, shanking and hooking them in alternate swats. I'd occasionally glance over at the pro who seemed uninterested enough to just watch a foursome come down on another fairway. After about ten hits I felt a presence off to my right. The presence spoke, "Try keeping your head down. Swing but just look at the ball." From there, at alternate ten ball hits, he'd show the correct grip, arm extension, hitting through the ball, and feet placement. Gradually the balls straightened and started to go down the center of the fairway. Afterward, I thought, "What a remarkable teacher." He must have seen a thousand things wrong during those first hits, but he chose the one appropriate thing to concentrate on; he said little but showed much as he took the club and showed the one thing to concentrate on.

I've given these two examples of learning episodes to show what I mean about writing down what went on. In Figure 6–1, you'll also see the kinds of things I've put in my inventory. Some of these may trigger memories of similar experiences you've had—the person and the learning event.

In exploring how I learn, sometimes I start in the middle column with people in my life. What did I learn from my Grandfather Hiller?—how to drive, sing, make pies, kill rats. During summer vacations I've learned from relatives and other people outside of school. I've also learned from my wife, my children, classroom teachers, and professors in seminary and graduate school.

Just as you write for ten minutes about an occasion, write an abbreviated account of a learning episode from your own learning chart. Try to show how both the teacher and you yourself are learning. Here are some ways to look at the episode after you've finished writing:

1. What worked? No matter how insignificant, try to remember the details as you write.
2. What were the problems?
3. How did the teacher select what to learn next?

ACTION: EXPERIMENT WITH LEARNING.

In this Action, you need to make a number of decisions before you start. The most important is choosing the learning episode or sequence that will work best for you.

1. *Simple learning episode.* This type of episode is one in which you can learn the skill or step in three to four hours or less: for example, try a new procedure in cooking, assemble something from directions, play a new game, or try a new dance step.
2. *Complex learning sequence.* Try to learn a series of Chinese cooking recipes, how to play the piano, bicycling, cross-country skiing, crocheting, ceramics, or working with wood, all of which involve an orchestrated sequence of skills.

The next decision is whether to work alone or choose a teacher. If possible, I strongly recommend choosing a teacher, especially if you're attempting the more complex learning sequence. In this way, you will be able to observe two processes, teaching and learning, instead of just learning. Choosing a teacher, however, requires some negotiation. Your teacher will need to know that you plan to share what is working and not working as you are being taught. This does not mean that your perceptions about learning will be correct, but it will give your teacher a chance to respond. You will also need to anticipate whether your teacher can handle the kind of frank response you need to give. Be sure to let your teacher know ahead of time that you want to report on what is working and what doesn't seem to work or what you don't understand so the teacher can adjust.

An even better structure for this Action would be mutual teaching and learning. For example, when I mentioned this notion to my wife, Betty, she said, "Oh good, you can teach me about basketball and I can teach you about using the sewing machine" (see the Action on p. 115). Mutual teaching makes for a more equitable balance in the teaching/learning situation. When I am teaching I will be much more conscious of what helps and doesn't help my partner and therefore more adept in responding as a learner. Above all, we must both be prepared to encounter very different approaches to learning. What helps one person doesn't help another.

The following episode is illustrative of teaching and learning by both teacher and student. (These excerpts are chosen from another book I am writing about teaching and learning.)

I've been cross-country skiing ten to a dozen times in my life. I've never broken through to any kind of proficiency. I'd heard about the new approach called "skating." Since I wasn't far enough along in the old way, I thought I'd try to learn; I asked my colleague, Jane Hansen, an accomplished skier and participant in fifty-kilometer marathons, to be my instructor.

The older way of skiing can best be described as a gliding shuffle in parallel tracks made by other skiers or a track-making machine. The new way, skating, has the skier moving like someone skating on ice with the glide carrying the ski outward at a forty-five-degree angle instead of in parallel in the old way. To watch a skier skate is to watch a graceful, seemingly effortless motion, with the skier leaning slightly into the step. "The Blue Danube Waltz" would be an appropriate accompaniment to the two-step motion. Good skiers can skate uphill as well as down.

I rented number 200 skis with Salomon bindings and headed for the snow-covered golf course. Hundreds of skiers were skiing but mostly in parallel. I had a funny feeling inside my stomach. As much as I like to learn, I don't like an audience when I'm learning.

"Watch me," Jane said, and gracefully skated off. Her skis pointed out and I wondered how she kept the backs from crossing over each other. Looked easy but I knew it wouldn't be.

I put my skis in the ruts and tried to push out in a skating motion with my right leg. I didn't fall, but I was as ungainly as a cow on ice. There was no skate to my motion. Jane skated back to check me out. I was beginning to resent her easy glide.

"Some people start by keeping one ski in the track and then just skate with the other one," Jane suggested.

"I've already tried that, but it didn't work very well," I replied. Since I was just starting, I kept on with the procedure. I pushed off again; I moved ahead, but I wasn't skating. Rather, my skiing now resembled a poorer version of parallel skiing.

"Push out like this," Jane shouted over her shoulder. "Keep your weight back so you can push out." Off she went again. I realized that watching her effortless motion hid all the little things I needed to know. My untrained eyes couldn't take in all that fluidity and make sense of it. I tried to keep my weight back and still had the one ski in the rut. But the ski that was to skate headed out from my body in a skating motion and kept right on going or stuck, and I'd waver back and forth struggling for balance; the skating motion was more remote than ever.

"Jane, I think you'd be better off watching me from behind instead of being in front. You take a look and see what's wrong." It was hard to ask her that, because I knew the sight would be pretty ugly. She looked and in a calm but definite voice said, "First thing in skating is you don't go with an every-other-ski-pole rhythm; they both go in at once." That helped a little, but the ruts were still bothering me.

"Jane, I'm going to get out of these ruts and see if that makes a difference." Even though I'd skied about a half mile, I still hadn't skated once. All I had was an ungainly, barbaric shuffle.

I pushed off on my right ski, turning the point like I'd seen Jane do. I also ignored the poles. Too complicated to bring them into the learning at this point. I needed to feel a skate stroke first, no matter how simple. At least that was my self-taught hunch. Jane changed her tactics too. She skied away, then back toward me, and then came up from behind. We were beginning to help each other circle the problems. When she skated toward me, I'd push a little for excellence, maybe try to hit a skate for two strokes. When she went away and couldn't see me, I'd experiment.

I also learned in my experimenting that my only chance for the feel of a skate was on a slight downhill. And it worked. I got in three good skates with my right leg. Jane skated toward me, laughing. "Don, you should see your mouth. You're concentrating so much your face and mouth are twisted to the right." The next day my right cheek and neck ached as they never had before. It was as if I'd slept in the wrong position. My face and mouth were trying to give my right skating leg some muscular support. I began to sense what stroke victims might go through.

"You know, Don, this takes time. Some people think you can just come out here and skate. It took me quite a long time to get it down, too, and I've been skiing for a while."

"Thanks, Jane. You don't have to tell me this is going to take time." I started off again, now catching the slight declines or flat places for my beginning skate, still not knowing what to do with my poles. I had absolutely no rhythm to anything. I had another thought. "Jane, I'm going to forget these poles for a while. I'll have *them or hold them for balance in case I'm going to fall. But I want to concentrate on just skating. No poles." It worked.*

I changed to another tactic. I was so pushy, wanting to make progress around the course, so afraid I'd be taken for some old fool, that I pushed harder for speed. I should have been working more for "slow feel." In fact, I was trying to go at the same speed as if I'd been skiing the old parallel way. "Forget speed; go for feel," I said to myself. That worked too. I noticed my tips gradually moving out from their old parallel position. I even got a skate in with my left foot. Three skates on both sides and suddenly, one stuck on a pebble or stick, and my three-skate confidence put me flat on my face, but my ego could handle falling now. I'd gotten in three skates.

Jane kept up her same pattern. Ski way off, look from behind to check my progress. I told her about the fall and sticking. "You'd probably be better off with real skating skis; you'd glide better, but on second thought, you'd have an even tougher time with speed." That made a lot of sense and fitted in with the notion that slower was better.

I decided to bring the poles back into the act. To this point I had skied slowly, pushing out for the feel of skating and holding my poles loosely but without really poling or pushing off. I tried pushing with them together but the rhythm just wasn't right. This time I looked at Jane up ahead. Now I knew a little more of what to look for. I noticed that her poles went with her right skate, which meant only a two count. I shifted to a two count. A skate with my right ski and push with the poles simultaneous to that. I shouted out loud, "Skate—two. Skate—two." I shouted to Jane. "Hey, I think this is it." I could feel the tips in the right place; I'd stick occasionally, even fall, and I couldn't skate uphill, but now four or five elements were beginning to come together.

"Most people don't get this the first time, you know." That may not be true, but I needed to hear it; I needed to hear it from her, the expert skier. At the age of fifty-six I needed to hear that my body could still learn things.

In this learning episode, Jane taught me about skiing and let me teach her about what was working and not working. We were both learners and teachers. She arranged her involvement so that she would be near enough to diagnose problems, yet able to move away to allow me to experiment. She let me talk and adjusted her teaching in return. Her suggestions were minimal—at the most, two at a time.

Learning episodes, like this example of learning to skate in cross-country skiing, can best be understood through intensive writing episodes of about thirty minutes. Even ten minutes of writing down what you recall will bring a harvest of understanding. Although I had some sense of what was going on during the skiing lesson, there was too much going on at the time to let me be aware of teaching and learning. Until I wrote about it, I didn't understand how Jane was teaching, the kind of space she gave me to learn, or how I had to learn to select and focus on the various components of skating. Once again, the value of writing is that it helps us see the world differently, above all by helping us learn how we learn.

In contrast to learning episodes, complex learning sequences last long enough for us to see how we put together more components. If I had continued my work with Jane I would look at the refinements that I needed to acquire over a three- or four-week period, depending on how often I could ski. Practicing skating once a day for five or six days could give me the kind of sequence I wanted. I'd want to record the changing roles of teacher and learner, and I suspect that if the learning was going well, the learner would supply more and more information to the teacher.

To get further insight into the teaching/learning, I'd write for ten minutes at that point where I thought there was the most information. My writing would be filled with as much detail as I could recall (recognizing that one detail begets more). Knowing that you plan to write after the learning episode heightens your intake of specifics. "I know I'll write about this part," you'll say, and your recall of details will begin right in the middle of your learning.

ACTION: TRY TO LEARN SOMETHING COMPLETELY NEW.

This Action takes courage. For this experiment, choose something that is conceptually foreign to you, something you've avoided learning most of your life. Put yourself in the place of the child who is breaking new ground.

As part of the experiment, choose a good teacher who will allow you to collaborate in the teaching and learning, as you did in the last Action. You will also ask your teacher if you may teach something you know that is new to him or her.

For this Action, I asked my wife, Betty, to teach me how to use the sewing machine. First, some background. I've only been a distant observer of the sewing scene. My mother sewed on her machine, first using the treadle, then an electric Singer in the forties. Betty sewed even more than Mother, making dress after dress for our four daughters. From time to time she'd call from the next room, "Come look at this dress. What do you think?" I'd look at the dress and nod approvingly, but ignore the machinery and the process she followed. The males in my generation of the Graves family have a genetic predisposition for ignoring the mechanical. We believe, as my father taught us, that touching machines and things electrical only makes matters worse.

My memories of thread and yarn are even more unhappy. In first grade, because of the John Dewey influence in the early thirties, I had to make an overcast stitch along the border of a piece of cloth, but I simply couldn't hold the needle so that the tip would even perforate the cloth, or if it did, I couldn't get it to come back through. Making a stitch an even distance from the edge along a whole side was simply beyond my reach. Overcasting was for me a debacle.

At the height of World War II, every student in our eighth grade, male or female, knitted squares, which were then connected into blankets for delivery to Great Britain. All good citizens had to do their part. I couldn't, and have suffered from mild guilt ever since when saluting the American flag. I'd knit ten stitches, drop two, regain my digital composure, and knit a few more. Three dismal, disorganized, bunched-up rows were my total production at the end of a week. Then Alice Winderknecht took pity on me and finished my square in fifteen minutes (I will remind her of her kindness at our fiftieth high school reunion in nine years).

Thus, learning to use a sewing machine was not a venture into the promised land. Still, in the spirit of pure experimentation, I learned. Here is what I wrote when I finished.

"This is a spool," Betty said, pointing to a spool of blue thread on the top of the machine. "The thread starts here. Now, if you want to know how the thread gets on here I can show you that."

"Better wait," I said. I could see that a long chain of moves lay ahead with the threading of the machine.

"Now take the thread and first move it through this hook, then down here, around this reel, snap it back so it catches, and then up here. . . ."

"Whoa, that's far enough," I said. "I'll never remember this. I think I can handle about four of those steps and that's all. I've got to try it, okay?" She let me thread the first five steps. My ability to clutch a thread hadn't changed since first grade. There is something completely foreign to me about fingering a thin thread between thumb and index finger. As I pondered the event I realized that I have no counterpart in my life for such fine motor activity. I've probably avoided every activity with thumb and index finger since my first-grade encounters with sewing. My whole body toiled. I felt the weight of threading the machine in my shoulders, neck, and lower back as those muscular reinforcements poured in to assist their inept cousins gripping the thin, blue line.

I found that remembering the steps for threading the machine was less difficult than the dexterity required. I had Betty do two sequences of about four steps, stop, then pull the thread out from the beginning so I'd be able to put the successful sequences end to end. It also gave me much-needed practice in holding the thread. I was surprised to find that the sequencing practice had improved my dexterity markedly by the time I had to thread the needle. With only two tries and much wetting of the thread end, I managed to thread the sewing machine needle. The bobbin underneath the machine took even less time, but I was surprised by my inability to handle cutting the thread on the hook behind the machine. That difficulty came from my own directive stubbornness.

"I've got to see what I'm doing to cut that thread," I barked to Betty. I stood up, leaned over the machine, adjusting my trifocals up and down to see the thread and cutting hook while holding the thread with both hands. I couldn't see the hook and my purchase was poor; the thread wouldn't cut.

"You don't need to see it at all. You have no leverage up there, just sit here, reach up behind the machine, and pull on that hook. You don't have to see," she repeated with finality. So much for helping someone teach. I was dead wrong and had to regroup. I sat as she commanded and easily cut the thread.

The sewing part was easy. I quickly got the feel of the machine's pulling the fabric and controlling the direction of the cloth, and my raising and lowering the presser foot. Within a few minutes I'd made a small pillow. "Just right for a gerbil," I remarked.

Betty chose to learn something equally foreign. For years she has heard me scream and moan from the next room while I watch the Boston Celtics play basketball on television. "You can teach me about basketball, but I want to interview you before watching any," she said as a condition of agreeing. The following is Betty's fifteen-minute, first-draft account of learning about the game of basketball.

Spectator sports held no interest for me growing up. The men I knew were so busy at farming, teaching, blacksmithing, home repairing, radio tinkering, and automobile maintenance that sports were not important. When there was time for play, they did the playing themselves—ice skating, swimming, sledding, mountain climbing, boating, etc. In my abstemious New England heritage, none of my forebears would waste money for admission to watch someone else play a sport. Add to the previous attitude my own dislike of beefy men showing off their physical strength and power to push others around, and you have a woman who will find lessons in understanding basketball difficult.

Nevertheless, Don and I sat down at the kitchen table, he with a pen and paper to draw diagrams and I with a scheme of questions in my mind that needed consecutive answers. Don drew a three-by-five inch rectangle for the court with the key and basket markings and put X's and O's for the two teams. Then I started the questioning, controlling the way he filled in the gaps in my information. What are the names of the players' positions? What are the markings on the floor called? What is the task of each player? Tell me about fouls. My questions continued, with Don supplying only the information I asked for. I was enjoying the answers arriving just as I needed them into the prereadied slots in my mind. Eventually we began to discuss the strategies of plays, how the men pass the ball from one to another, how they guard and press.

At this point I'm getting confused and can't remember all the details. I'm asking for repeat information.

Don has a helpful suggestion. "Let's watch the UCLA–Washington State game; it's on TV now." Time to apply my new knowledge.

It is extremely hard for me to interpret all the jangled motion on the screen at one time. I want to know why they call a foul, why the blue team got possession of the ball. How come the blues get three points for that basket? I am annoyed when my husband discusses the plays with his father and my questions are not immediately answered. I want control.

Don has another helpful suggestion. "Just watch one player." As I begin to follow #23 on the blue UCLA team, the game starts to come alive. I get my first spark of enthusiasm; I can participate in the comments going back and forth between Don and his dad. I am delighted when #23 makes a basket.

In the past my only goal for TV sports events was to get them over as soon as possible, shut the TV off as soon as my husband finished watching it, and return to the normal activities of daily living. On this night I am amazed to hear myself demanding that the men turn the TV back on so that I can hear the postgame discussion and learn if my #23 was chosen most valuable player for the game. He was not! All I can say is "the officials" were not watching #23 as carefully as I, and they missed his brilliant strategies.

FINAL REFLECTION   Learning is such a serious matter that we have to know how to laugh in the midst of it. Serious matters show all too clearly our human foibles, and to those who are continually learning, most foibles inspire laughter. When Jane skied toward me and mentioned the twisted, distorted look on the right side of my face, it broke the tension of my overly serious preoccupation with learning to skate on skis. One of the reasons it is so important for us to practice learning is to have a clearer picture of ourselves, clear enough to be able to laugh with the children at our mutual attempts to learn. Laughter helps me to relax and gives me the confidence to try again.

Teachers who know how to listen, who incorporate the details of their observations and experience in their spoken and written language, have the tools to know how to celebrate learning. Celebrations can be as simple as a well-timed smile when both teacher and learner share an awareness that something good has happened. When it's time to celebrate, both teacher and learner, who have struggled hard to reach an objective, rest a moment and savor with a whoop or a laugh the "crossing of the bar."

It's hard to write about celebration. After several tries, I still haven't got my finger on it. I've seen teachers like Mary Ellen Giacobbe, Nancie Atwell, Pat McLure, and Leslie Funkhouser

lean back and laugh, or say, "Isn't it wonderful; you've finished, you've done it!" I was present when John, a first grader,
beamed as he read back a page, and his teacher, Mary Ellen
Giacobbe, said in celebration, "John, you're reading. That's
what you just did." Her tone was joyfully celebratory. Byrd
Baylor's *I'm in Charge of Celebrations* is a good book to read just
to get the feel of what celebratory living is all about. I mention
humor and celebration because both are an essential part of a
classroom environment in which children successfully sur-
mount learning problems. Laughter and a joyful sense of
achievement ease the way as children learn to seek solutions
to the new "bugs" they encounter.

Through practice—and through literate engagement—I learn
to watch myself learn in many life-related events. I practice,
talk and write, then practice again until I understand myself
and the processes of learning. When I do this, I enrich my own
life and celebrate being alive, and I bring that same joy at en-
countering the new into my own classroom. Teaching and
learning are inseparable events, two sides of one process. I
work overtime to help children become better teachers so that
they can make these powerful tools their own.

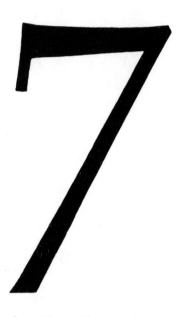

look ahead

You may have arrived at this point in the book after a quiet evening of reading, perhaps to find out what might be involved in the concept *"discover your own literacy."* If so, you have already decided which Actions you are ready to try. It is also possible that you began this book in September and it is now April, that you decided to try a chapter a month, moving slowly through the various Actions.

It was my intention to make this a slow-paced book with a minimum of reading and a maximum of experimenting. For me many of these Actions required several years of exploration, and some demand lifelong dedication. The final goal is not total mastery, but rather, the lifelong wonder of learning.

I've tried to help all of us rediscover our own literacy. It certainly was something I needed to do for myself. Although I have written books and done some reading, I found that the process of participating in the Actions included here has given me a new view of myself and the world around me.

The idea for this book was triggered by my observations of teachers who have made a major difference in their classrooms. When I travel around the country (in the course of the last six or seven years I've been in two-thirds of the states), I frequently visit classrooms, and one thing is clear: children want to read and write. Their writing folders are filling up, and they read books if given the opportunity. Classrooms are places of interest and energy. But I have sensed a threshold of achievement beyond which a majority of children do not pass.

If children are to cross that threshold and demonstrate a higher quality of literate engagement than we have seen before, teachers' literacy will have to change as well. Teachers like Nancie Atwell, Linda Rief, and Mary Ann Wessells are themselves insatiable learners. By demonstrating how they learn to their children, they encourage the children to learn in the same way. Their literate engagement looks for answers to questions that are much larger than those in the curriculum mandated in U.S. school systems. They listen, read, and write in order to understand the world around them—for themselves. But their literacy and learning also provide a backdrop for what the children do and serve as an open invitation to them to explore the wonder, complexity, and mystery in the world around them. Although as teachers your professional lives are centered in the children, you first need to read, write, listen, and learn for yourself.

It's time to look ahead. I want to explore the next steps for continuing our growth in literacy and for inviting children to join us. First, plan your own continuing involvement in literacy.

PLAN SOME SHARING

I keep my literacy alive when I know people with whom I can share. I have a select few: my wife, Betty; Don Murray; Jane Hansen; Nancie Atwell; Mary Ellen Giacobbe. Chances are, one or two of them will read a healthy share of the pieces I write. If I am writing something, no matter how short, trivial, or extensive, I'll probably tuck it in the mail, read it over the phone, or plan a short lunch. Sometimes I suspect that one of my pieces is not only poorly written but boring, or even a waste of time. Although I'd prefer otherwise, there is always an amount of risk for us both in what I pass along. But we need friends who can handle that, and we need to do the same for them.

Most of our literate communities are cultivated; that is, just as we saw in Chapter 6, we need to help other people know what helps us. We send signals that are fairly specific when we give someone a piece of writing, although our need for help with a particular piece can vary enormously. Here are a few samples of requests for help (the reasons for each request are in italic):

- Listen to this and don't say anything when I'm done. I just want an audience. I need a face, a human being who is here. No more.

Sometimes I don't want any help at all, just a friendly ear, so that I can hear my own voice as I read.

- Listen to this. I'd like you to say what this is about, what you remember. No more than that.
  This is probably the most important and common directive to a reader. Notice that I don't ask, "What do you think of this?" or, "Is this any good?" The quality of the piece is revealed more by what the person can actually say she understands or what she will do and how she'd do it. As I listen to the person's response, I judge whether this is what I want her to understand.

- Listen to this. Tell me what this is about. Then tell me what is clearest to you and what isn't so clear.
  This directive requires more of the reader. If I think I have a reader who can handle this, I'll ask it. Above all, notice that I am setting the reader up to get what I want. That's my job, to sense what will help me and try to show someone else how to provide that information.

- Would you please read this and tell me what this is about?
  In this instance I want the reader to decide what the main thrust of the piece is. Sometimes I think I already know, but I'm so close to the piece I can't tell. There are some instances in which I'll tell the reader what I think it is about and then ask him to read and tell me what he thinks, but I prefer the former approach.

- Would you please read this, decide what the piece is about, and then find the place, the story, or the image that most reveals it?
  Sometimes my best material doesn't appear until much later in the piece. It's often hard for me to know what strikes a reader most forcefully, or which material is best and belongs up front.

- Would you please read this and mark the places that just don't make sense? Even if you just wonder what they mean, please underline them.
  Asking a reader to underline the "fuzzy" places is a good preliminary for help in editing. This should precede any attention to spelling, punctuation, or grammatical problems. Until I deal

with the issues in logic I am wasting a friend's time asking for judgments about surface features.

- Would you please read this and check any "errors" that will turn a reader off?

   This particular request comes at the end of the process, when I am sending a piece off or going to press. I make this request after I have gone as far as I can on my own and after I have dealt with other issues.

We create our own learning communities by preparing others to help us. There are many kinds of audiences to consider. If you wanted help on a piece that was of a technical nature or pertained to teaching, you'd most likely ask another teacher to comment. On the other hand, I often ask a good layperson, a person outside the field, to comment as well. I should be writing clearly enough for laypeople to understand me. But if that person asks, "What's this word, what does this part mean?" I probably haven't written well enough for a professional audience.

ACTION: CHOOSE ONE OR TWO PIECES TO SHARE.

Look over your collection of pieces on literate occasions or what you may have written during the Actions and share several with another person. Think over what you think you need help with and ask someone to provide the assistance you'd like. In fact, ask more than one person to get a sense of how your requests are working.

ACTION: WRITE ABOUT ONE OR TWO OCCASIONS TO SHARE WITH CHILDREN.

Some of our best audiences are the children in our classrooms. Practice asking them to respond to specific pieces, or at different phases of the writing process. Students ought to see that you are writing, and they can practice giving help.

ACTION: LOOK AHEAD TO WHAT YOU'D LIKE TO LEARN.

Make a list of specific skills you'd like to learn outside of school. As I look at my list, I realize that I used to do many of the things on it rather well but have simply allowed my skills to gather dust. For example, I'd like to get back to photography. It's been about twelve years since I've done it seriously—actually taking a camera with me wherever I go. I'd need to shoot three or four rolls of film a week just to begin to see again. I'd also need to reactivate my basement darkroom. I'd also like to get back to spending more time observing birds, which would actually be easier than reclaiming photography. Look back to something you used to enjoy and plan some way to bring it to life again for yourself.

Try looking ahead to something you'd like to learn. I've noted some of the activities my friends do well, and cooking is one of them. I enjoy working in the kitchen, but I've never considered it in a serious way. Yes, I'd like to explore that area.

As you go over your list, consider finding someone to try some of these new areas of learning with you.

By now, you may be wondering how on earth a sane person can consider all these possibilities. Perhaps you've said, "I'll have to retire just to do Chapter 7." But as in the other chapters, the intent of the Actions in this chapter is to provide you with options for continuing your own literate engagement. You may decide to choose only one Action as the focus for maintaining freshness in your literate activity.

Your choice, in most cases, will involve you in far more sharing with others. In the writing Action you made it a point to share your writing on a continuing basis. You worked at helping others help you. In the next Action you will share your reading.

ACTION: FORM A GROUP TO SHARE BOOKS.

There can be no more joyful or informative way of maintaining our personal and professional lives than sharing the books we are reading. This is especially true if you have provided extended opportunities for the children in your classroom to read books (see Chapter 4).

Reinvigorate your reading by forming a small book group. Designate a time once a week—it need not be longer than an hour. Find two or three teachers who will agree to set aside an hour after school. You can have as many as six, but the larger the group, the more difficult it will be to schedule and maintain the discipline that goes with sharing. Meet at the school, or better still, meet in a restaurant or home near the school, where you can get away, sip some coffee or tea, perhaps nibble a few snacks, and talk informally about books.

There are many ways to discuss books. The most important thing is to have conversations about them, much as you'd talk about your children on the telephone. What strikes you? What makes you wonder? Read aloud your favorite parts; share the language that delights you. If your group has more than four or five it is helpful to have one person who is responsible for ensuring balanced participation.

All books deserve to be shared: mystery and detective novels, the classics, historical novels, modern novels, collections of short stories, poetry, biography, and autobiography. The most obvious are the very books the children read in school. I find that a discussion of children's literature often leads to questions and insight as great as any with books for adults.

Occasionally the group may wish to read the same book together. Or you may each choose to read a different book by the same author or books in the same genre: historical or biographical novels, detective stories, or children's picture books.

FINAL REFLECTION
We've planned ways to sustain our rediscovery of literacy. Now that I've been able to rediscover literacy for myself, I want to keep alive this new relationship with the universe. I do so by continuing to write, read, and listen to myself. Most of the time, this means sharing with others and listening to friends,

who explore the world in their own ways. Our dialogue helps me to be more aware of my opinions and the evidence that backs up my thinking. Obviously, we need to allow children the same opportunities we've discovered for ourselves. But there is no guarantee that this will happen.

Nancie Atwell tells the story of a teacher and mother who provided her son with a rich environment for literacy and learning at home. There were children's books, crafts, paper, and all kinds of writing instruments. She enjoyed reading for herself, and she read to her child and had him work next to her as they experimented with crafts together. When her son went to school he was already an avid reader and a good, independent thinker. Yet she told her child's teacher that she was mystified about her son's abilities and saw no connection between her role and the joy her child knew in learning. And sadly, she did not permit the children in her own classroom to have the same rich experience she provided for her son. She read no literature to her children, didn't let them write, and fed them a diet of skill sheets and basal readers. She was an intelligent, literate human being who saw no connection between her own literate life as a mother and what her own students needed in school.

We've had a different experience. Although this book stresses literacy for us as teachers, we have found that when children are allowed to read trade books in school, to write and listen, the quality of their literacy parallels ours. They become critical of themselves and the world around them, discovering at the same time the wonder of the universe.

references

Atwell, Nancie. 1984. "Writing and Reading Literature from the Inside Out." *Language Arts* 61 (3) (March).

———. 1987. *In the Middle: Writing, Reading, and Learning with Adolescents.* Portsmouth, N.H.: Boynton/Cook.

Baylor, Byrd. 1978. *The Other Way to Listen.* New York: Charles Scribner and Sons.

———. 1986. *I'm in Charge of Celebrations.* New York: Macmillan.

Bianco, Margery Williams. 1971. *Velveteen Rabbit.* Garden City, NY: Doubleday.

Byars, Betsy C. 1984. *The Computer Nut.* New York: Viking.

Campbell, Joseph, and Bill Moyers. 1988. *The Power of Myth.* New York: Doubleday.

Dahl, Roald. 1985. *The B.F.G.* New York: Penguin.

Frankl, Victor E. 1984. *Man's Search for Meaning: An Introduction to Logotherapy.* 3rd ed. New York: Simon & Schuster.

Graves, Donald H. 1983. *Writing: Teachers & Children at Work.* Portsmouth, N.H.: Heinemann.

Hall, Donald. 1986. *The Happy Man.* New York: Random House.

Hansen, Jane. 1987. *When Writers Read.* Portsmouth, N.H.: Heinemann.

Irving, Washington. 1963. *Rip Van Winkle and the Legend of Sleepy Hollow.* Illustrated by David Levine. New York: Macmillan.

L'Engle, Madeleine. 1970. *A Wrinkle in Time.* New York: Farrar, Straus & Giroux.

———. 1973. *A Wind in the Door.* New York: Farrar, Straus & Giroux.

Paterson, Katherine. 1977. *Bridge to Terabithia.* New York: Harper & Row.

Thomas, Lewis. 1975. *The Lives of a Cell: Notes of a Biology Watcher.* New York: Bantam.

———. 1979. *The Medusa and the Snail: More Notes of a Biology Watcher.* New York: Viking.

White, E. B. 1952. *Charlotte's Web.* New York: Harper & Row.

index

Actions, 15; abolishing reading groups, 53–55; choosing pieces to share, 126; difficult listening occasions, 97–98; experiment with learning, 109–15; finding readers, 35; forming a group to share books, 127–28; helping children learn to listen, 100–102; helping children write about books, 55–77; letting children read, 48–53; letting children share in your reading, 78; listening for children's voices, 94–95; listening to own voice, 85–93, 94; looking ahead to what you'd like to learn, 127–28; looking for children's voices, 94–95; making decisions about, 17–18; plan to evolve as listener, 99–100; practicing when not to listen, 95–97; reading aloud to children, 46–48; rethinking skills, 77–78; reviewing own learning history, 106–9; sharing reading with others, 45–46, 128–29; sharing with children, 126; starting to read, 42–45; taking

advantage of literate occasions, 22–24; trying to learn something completely new, 115–19
Aegis, 10
Atwell, Nancie, 21, 35, 48–49, 56, 119, 123, 124, 129
Audiences, 83–84

Bailey, Janis, 56
Basal readers, 39–40, 50–51, 109
Baylor, Byrd, 43, 52, 120
Book groups, 128–29
Books: analyzing, 41–42; children's journals about, 55–56; choosing, 42–43, 52–53; letting children choose, 48–53; reading, 43–45; sharing, 40, 52, 78; sharing (Action), 128–29. *See also* Reading

Campbell, Joseph, 89–93
Celebration, learning and, 119–20
Children: difficult listening occasions with (Action), 98; encouraging reading by, 48–53, 129; helping to listen (Action), 100–102; interest in learning of, 123; journal-keeping by, 55–56; letters about books by, 55–77; limits on